"Having spent some thirty years listening to and witnessing my patients' pain, I am more than familiar with what makes people miserable. This book is the outgrowth of my curiosity about what makes people happy. How are happy people different from those who have sought my help? What common threads run through the stories of *their* lives?"

DR. HAROLD GREENWALD is the founder and director of the Direct Decision Therapy Institute, and chairman of the Psychology Department at the United States International University in San Diego. He maintains a prestigious private practice, and has authored six books, including *Direct Decision Therapy, Active Psychotherapy, Great Cases in Psychoanalysis, Emotional Maturity in Love and Marriage*, and the best-selling classic, *The Call Girl.*

ELIZABETH RICH is the author of three books, including *Flying High*, which has sold more than a half-million copies.

The Happy Person

A SEVEN-STEP PLAN

DR. HAROLD GREENWALD
AND ELIZABETH RICH

AVON
PUBLISHERS OF BARD, CAMELOT, DISCUS AND FLARE BOOKS

AVON BOOKS
A division of
The Hearst Corporation
1790 Broadway
New York, New York 10019

The Stein and Day edition contains the following Library of
Congress Cataloging in Publication Data:

Greenwald, Harold, 1910-
   The happy person.

   1. Decision-making—Psychological aspects.
2. Happiness. 3. Choice (Psychology) I. Rich, Elizabeth.
II. Title.
BF441.G74   1984   153.8′3   83-40347

First Avon Printing, February, 1985

For my grandchildren who have helped make me a happy person: Abraham, Anna, Leah, and Rachel

HG

For Nikos, who supports my decisions with love and understanding and never complains when I choose to be with the typewriter

ER

ACKNOWLEDGMENTS

First I want to extend, in print, my special thanks to my co-author, Elizabeth Rich, who has made this book the happiest I have written.

My thanks, also, go to the expert editorial help provided by Renni Browne and staff members of The Editorial Department, especially John Maloney.

Bob Stokesberry got me started on this path, and I thank him for his great help and friendship.

Special thanks for her long and arduous support go to my agent, Jane Jordan Browne.

Last but not least, thank you to my many students who helped me with research and interviews—and, as always to my enduring wife, Ruth.

CONTENTS

1

The Lady or the Tiger

THERE is a tribe on Papua New Guinea known as the Cargo Cult.* For decades these people have been waiting for a great bird to swoop down from the clouds and drop riches and magical gifts on them. Their whole lives revolve around complicated rituals to make this happen. They are, quite literally, waiting for happiness to drop from the sky.

They're not as crazy as they seem. During World War II, huge airplanes did drop boxes of food and magical gifts ranging from mirrors to jeeps. Sometimes they dropped bombs. After the war, a tribal headman made the decision to recreate the wartime conditions and lure back the first big bird. So at every harvest, these people burn almost all their crops. Periodically they destroy their villages, too. Most of the men refuse to work at all, keeping a constant vigil.

Now this decision has been operative for an entire tribe of people for over forty years. And the Cargo Cult isn't just an oddity, either; it's a monumental headache to the government of Papua New Guinea—sometimes the cult members get frustrated and burn other tribes' crops and villages as well as their own. Reasonable explanations make no impression whatsoever. They continue to wait and burn. They are not known to be happy people.

---

* *Road Below Cargo*, Peter Lawrence, Melbourne University Press, 1964.

There is another tribe, called the Senoi, who live on the Malay Peninsula. According to Kilton Stewart, these people get a special pleasure in life from interpreting their dreams. Every morning the families discuss their dreams and then take their most interesting ones to the village council.

One method they have devised for dealing with children's nightmares is to encourage the child to recreate the dream every night until the monster can be coaxed into giving him a gift. The parents help the child discover how his courage and patience can eventually tame the monster. Once the gift has been received, the nightmare is then turned into a wonderful dream. The Senoi are known to be very happy people.

The life circumstances of these two primitive tribes are essentially similar. It's the way they experience their lives that is so different. Members of the Cargo Cult are brought up to believe that there can be no happiness without the appearance of that "no-show" bird. Their experience of their lives is, not surprisingly, one of deprivation and dissatisfaction.

The Dream People have an entirely different "mind set." It's as if they have tuned their sets to a wonderful television station offering fascinating nightly programs they can use to expand and enrich their lives every day.

Like most psychotherapists, I have spent a great deal of time studying unhappy people, carefully exploring with my patients their cargoes of trauma, frustration, and defeat. Most of the literature I have read in the field is similarly devoted to the analysis of misery.

A number of years ago I became aware of some profound contradictions in my preparation as a therapist. On the one hand, I was making myself an expert on sorrow; on the other hand, I could see that my sorrowful patients, like most people, were searching for some form of happiness—even if, like Schopenhauer, they defined it as the absence of pain.

Schopenhauer and quite a few others have found it easier to define happiness by saying what it isn't than by saying what it is. If you look "happiness" up in the dictionary, you're likely to be disappointed. Yet I am convinced that we all have a private definition of happiness—a way of being in the world seen as tranquil or fulfilling or exciting or powerful or satisfying or loving or connected or independent. . . . The list could go on and on, which of course is the point: neither I nor anyone else can tell you what makes you happy.

Having spent some thirty years listening to and witnessing my patients' pain, I am more than familiar with what makes people miserable. This book is, among other things, the outgrowth of my curiosity about what makes people happy. How are happy people different from those who have sought my help? What common threads run through the stories of *their* lives?

During this study I have made a number of fascinating discoveries. The most surprising was how many of the joyous, satisfied people I interviewed for this book had undergone traumas, frustrations, and defeats remarkably similar to my misery-laden patients. The same circumstances, I found, can provide one person with reason for deepest despair and another with a source of amusement.

A famous surgeon I met at a party told me a story that dramatically illustrates this truth. Having built a holiday vacation house overlooking Big Sur, he then lent it to a newly married couple before he had spent so much as a night in it himself. The couple bought a broom and dustpan to clean up the wood shavings left by the carpenters, started a cozy fire in the living room fireplace, then went off for a swim in the Pacific. When they got back, they found the house burned to the ground.

The next week, the surgeon received a bill for $3.95 from the husband—for the broom and dustpan.

More startling than the story itself was the way the surgeon told it. "It was years ago," he said, "and I still laugh when I remember getting that bill in the mail. All the bother with the insurance people, the cleaning up, and the decisions, decisions about the whole mess—somehow all of that began to seem insignificant compared to how important the $3.95 was to the husband. You know, the more I realized that the $3.95 did make a difference to him, the more I realized how fortunate I was. The loss of the whole house really didn't make that kind of difference to me at all. And what a great story I have to tell! The broom and dustpan have become priceless in my memory."

In mine, too. I remember the surgeon whenever I am tempted to cast myself as a victim in the story of my own life. Most people, myself included, would have wound up that story something like this: "And do you know what they had the nerve to do to me after all of that?" Not the surgeon. His experience of the whole sequence of events was totally different because he refused to see himself as a victim. He *chose*, in fact, to see himself along entirely different lines.

Happy people seem to do this naturally, often turning their problems on their heads, using them to advantage. I interviewed a woman who was told by her doctor that she had inoperable cancer and six months at most to live. Among her reactions to this piece of news was a truly extraordinary one: "a sense of relief," as she described it to me.

"Suddenly the future was something I didn't have to worry about anymore. I didn't have to worry about what I *had* to do—I could do anything I damned well pleased. I had six months' worth of minutes left, and I was going to enjoy every single one of them."

The story almost has an unhappy ending. The doctor was wrong. When she went to see him a few months later, there was no trace of cancer.

"For a few moments," she told me, "I felt overwhelmed all over again by the responsibilities I used to worry about. And then I realized: the same thing is waiting for all of us, whether in a year or in fifty years. If I could be so happy living every moment in my last six months to the hilt, I could do the same thing however much time I had left."

And she did. To this day she perceives her life as a gift—a perception frequently fundamental to the way happy people see their lives.

People who impress us with unexpected, inspiring reactions to the disasters in their lives become a little larger than life in memory. What's more, we have an opportunity to learn something valuable about ourselves whenever someone demonstrates that moment of choice for us. It is indeed a magical moment—like the one when the magician pulls out the cut-up scarf intact and silky, floating through the air.

What such a moment enables us to see is the possibility of performing an act of magic on ourselves. Of choosing the happy alternative—to be enriched rather than devastated when *our* next calamity or disappointment comes along.

The happy people I interviewed in preparing this book had all chosen not to be victims, whether they realized it or not. In other words, they had chosen to be happy. Granted, for some of them the choice had been a logical outcome of fortunate circumstances. But only for a very small percentage. Most often the decision was made on the heels of a severe emotional or physical crisis in their lives—a near-fatal accident, or a disastrous divorce, or the agonizing realization that life up to that point had, in one way or another, been self-destructive or simply unrewarding.

Now these are clearly the circumstances many sad people use to explain their unhappiness. *So why weren't these people sad?*

Again and again I found that they made use of such circumstances to reexamine their way of looking at the world, their way of *being* in the world. They then decided, consciously or unconsciously, that they were responsible for their own happiness.

Victims don't do that. And if there's one thing my experience as a psychotherapist has taught me, it is that no one has to be a victim. However important external factors like health, physical appearance, and upbringing may be, they don't have to determine the happiness quotient in anyone's life story. The way we experience our lives is, quite simply, up to us.

In the late nineteen-sixties I began to put together a method of brief therapy to help unstick my patients from their swamps of unhappiness. I even wrote a book about it—*Direct Decision Therapy*. As it has evolved since then, from my ongoing experience with patients and with the people I interviewed for this book, the therapy has addressed itself more and more to the question of happy alternatives.

The more people I talk to, the clearer it becomes to me that we *decide* how we are going to experience the world—whether we're aware of our operative decision or not. And our reactions in turn determine our actions or future behavior, which almost always has predictable consequences, and these consequences generate their own predictable reactions . . .

And so it goes. Which means that if you can unearth your operative decisions, you can fairly accurately predict what you are going to get out of life. When any of us sees that no one but ourselves made the choice, the conclusion is obvious: we got what we wanted. Only after we can see our role as the decision maker can we see our way to choosing something different—like happiness, if it happens to be missing.

Now all of this didn't come to me like a thunderbolt from the Great God of Mental Health. I learned it, bit by bit, from my patients and students. (The amount I learn from them is a great fringe benefit of being a psychotherapist and teacher.) Although I admire Sir Edmund Hillary as the man who, in his own words, "conquered Mount Everest," I prefer the way his Sherpa, Tensing Norgay, described the experience: "The mountain and I together attained the heights."

The happy people I interviewed had not conquered themselves. I suspect that it may be impossible to conquer one's self without getting blood all over the floor, and I'm certain that people at war with themselves aren't happy. A gentler and more inviting goal, in the words of Nietzsche, might be "taming our demons and turning them into divine children." Or, if not our children, at least our gift-bearing friends, like the Dream People's.

I just want you to know that you, like the Dream People, have the power to change channels if you want to. On your own or with professional help, the truth about you—whoever you are—is that you carry within yourself the resources to heal your most grievous pain, overcome your most paralyzing fears, devise ingenious solutions to your most burdensome problems.

If you have read this far, you obviously have some interest in what makes people happy. In these pages you will meet the happy men and women I interviewed, along with patients whose experiences illuminate some of the dark closets of unawareness we all wander into from time to time. All of these people—the patients and the nonpatients—ended up in a similar state: happy and fulfilled. (I'm saving the case histories of those who chose to stay miserable for another book.)

But what if happiness is already at hand? Why then should you—or I—become aware of the choices that determine how we experience our lives?

There's a very good reason why. As long as we are breathing, life can turn the tables on us. You might look upon this book, then, as a sort of psychic insurance. The happy people I interviewed often reported back to me that the interviews had clarified their sense of their lives and their own role in choosing the happy alternative.

My profession, of course, brings me people who have a great gift for choosing the *un*happy alternative. As in the story of the Lady or the Tiger, they are likely to throw open the wrong door and be overwhelmed by tigers. They come to me because they hope I can give them some clues for choosing the safer door. They think I know what the Lady looks like.

What I have learned from happy people is not that they are lucky enough to open the right door always. They aren't. They see their share of tigers. It's just that the moment they see the tiger's green eyes, they decide to become wild animal tamers.

2

Steps in the
Right Direction

DIRECT Decision Therapy, as I originally conceived it and as it has evolved through my interviews with happy people for this book, is a form of "brief therapy." Although traditional therapy works some of the time for some patients, it doesn't work all of the time. And even when it does work, it takes a long time and costs a lot of money. That's why those forms of therapy that produce their results more quickly have gained more and more acceptance—from the 48-hour marathon encounters of the sixties to behavior modification to the currently popular three-months-on-the-couch.

Many psychotherapists, psychiatrists, and psychoanalysts still believe that therapy isn't valuable unless it's a lengthy, leisurely process. They forget that most of the leaders and founders of the American Psychoanalytic Association were themselves originally trained by Freud in one-month analyses in Vienna during their vacations. And even these diehards will admit that, very often, extended therapy provides a patient with a means to avoid reaching any kind of decision he then would have to carry out.

Most people who come to see a therapist—of whatever school—will be asked in the first session to state why they want help. The assumption is that they come to discuss their problems. My interviews with nonpatients for this book have brought about a change in the way I approach my prospective patients. Now, in the first session, I often say something like, "Do you want me to concentrate on your problems or would you like us to work together on making you happy?"

Viewing happiness as an achievable goal often gives patients the confidence and energy to deal constructively with their problems from the very beginning of therapy. I'm still amazed at how much time it can save.

Sometimes the question by itself can set a patient on the right track. I remember one man who came to see me, so involved with his work that he was in a constant state of crisis over how much he had to do. Not only that, but he had two girlfriends and was in agony over which one to choose.

He'd been through five years of analysis with another therapist, and was clearly up for another five years with me. "Before we go any farther," I said, "how about forgetting all these terrible problems for a moment and looking at what might make you happy?"

At first his unhappy self chattered away at him—and he chattered away at me—about all those problems.

"I'm serious," I said. "Wouldn't you like to be happy?"

He finally heard me and smiled. "Yes. I'd like that."

So I asked him, "Okay, what can you do to be happy?"

"Dr. Greenwald," he said, "*nobody* could be happy with the amount of work I have to do, the responsibilities I have. There's just not enough of me to go around. And then, when I finally get home from work, I need recreation, and let me tell you, recreation isn't the way to describe trying to please two women. One would be plenty, and I just can't choose between them—they're both wonderful."

"Okay," I said. "Maybe we can start by looking at your life in a different way. For one thing, you have a very successful business, which could be a real source of satisfaction in your life. It's creative and challenging and you're obviously good at it. The problem is, you allow *it* to drive *you* instead of allowing yourself to enjoy *it*. Is that true?"

He said it was true, and after a few sessions he started coming up with ways he could slow down and enjoy his business instead of saying yes to every potential client, which left him always feeling behind. Having progressed in the work area, we moved on to his love life. "So you're involved with these two terrific women," I said, "and both of them think *you're* terrific. This is a tragedy?"

He laughed.

"So, how about enjoying the situation if you can't decide between them at the moment?"

Now, we proceeded to go through the Direct Decision steps, pretty much as they are laid out in this chapter. But the number of sessions it took for him to convince himself that his terrible problems could be very rewarding situations—and, therefore, to experience his life as very rewarding—amounted to "brief" therapy. Why? Because he quickly was able to redefine the situations that had brought him to me in the first place. His problems disappeared without our having to figure out what trauma in his childhood had led him to be the sort of man who creates such impossible problems for himself.

This all may strike you as absurdly simple, and if you really want your life to be complicated, this approach isn't for you. But what this patient and many other patients proved to me is that, given the choice to be happy, many unhappy people are able to decide that happiness is what they want. Then, like the people I interviewed for this book, they develop the ability to experience their problems in a different way.

If you see a situation in your life as a problem, then that's what it is—a problem. If you see it as an opportunity, it can suddenly look and feel very different.

A lot of my fellow professionals will find this approach not just absurdly simple, but simply absurd. I had some trouble with myself on this score: one of the really important things I had to do in order to make Direct Decision Therapy possible was to decide, for myself, that it could be done. Unfortunately, when a therapist believes strongly that it is impossible for any therapy to be effective except in a long, extended relationship, he communicates this belief to the patient. Then, of course, therapy takes a long, long time.

Now your problems may require professional help, perhaps even extended professional help. If so, get the help you need. But if you're like most people, you can get a lot more happiness into your life by deciding that you want to be happy and taking some uncomplicated steps to make happiness possible for you.

For professionals and nonprofessionals alike, the best way to learn any therapeutic technique is to apply the therapy to yourself. (The most valuable part of my training as an analyst was my own psychoanalysis.) If you're interested in learning Direct Decision Therapy, you can apply it to yourself as you read about it.

In this chapter I give an overview of the specific steps that make up the technique. There are seven of them, but the therapy could just as well be explained in ten steps, or five steps, or no steps at all. I've simply broken down what I do as a therapist into seven steps, and devoted a chapter to each one. My intention is to make it easier for you to be your own therapist.

I. Decide What You Want in Order to Be Happy (or Happier)

That's it, that's the first step. Okay, so you want to be happy: what does that mean to you? What do you really want? If you're asking yourself that question right now, you may already have realized that this isn't always as easy as it sounds.

"I want to stop being self-destructive."
"I want to find some meaning in life."
"I want to fulfill my potential."

These are all too general. Keep asking yourself "What, exactly, do I want?"

I remember Susan, a young woman who gave all of the above responses when I asked her what she wanted.

"All right," I said, "now what does all that mean to you? What do you really want?"

"I want to find a husband."

Wonderful! Suddenly the goal was clear and we had something to work with. In chapter 3, I'll give you more help with answering this question for yourself.

II. Find the Decision Behind the Problem

Once you have defined your goal in specific terms, the next thing is to describe the problems you have in reaching that goal. In the case of Susan, who wanted to find a husband, the problem was that all the men she became involved with were irresponsible, unreliable, and very often already married. She agreed that it was she who had picked these men and that each one further confirmed her opinion: all men are no-good liars who will leave you.

Now we get to a tricky part. The admission that she was the one who chose these men gave her a perfect opportunity to become even more depressed about not finding a husband. She could really feel hopeless about being so stupid, so sick. Then there would be nothing to stop her from going out and choosing yet another irresponsible, unreliable man who'd tell her lies and then leave her. The judge who sits inside us all, you see, is a hanging judge.

When Susan was very young, I learned, her father had abandoned the family and her mother had turned bitter and resentful of men in general. This situation was what led up to Susan's *operative decision*—the decision underlying her self-defeating behavior. She decided, as a child, that men were no-good liars who would leave her—and then proceeded as a young woman to fall for men who would prove her right.

Please understand that this was not a brilliant deduction arrived at through the creative process. The first rule I follow whenever I'm doing Direct Decision Therapy is to empty my mind of everything I know about psychology. (This rule was very hard to follow when I was starting out and didn't know much. It's much easier now that I know a lot more.) I forget everything I know about neurosis, psychosis, transference, and all the rest of the jargon, and ask myself, "What is this person telling me?" In short, I listen. I listen hard because only then can I discover what that person is experiencing. If you listen hard to yourself, you can unearth your own operative decision.

If I'm following this rule, I don't have to worry too much about the other: don't judge. In my time, I have had people walk into my office and describe some outrageous, destructive behavior, but if I listen hard enough I won't be tempted to judge the behavior—I'll understand it, I won't judge it. After all, if I can't suspend my judgment, there's no hope of my helping the patient.

So my advice to you is to call upon the good therapist in yourself to send the hanging judge out to lunch. We don't care whether he thinks you're stupid or wicked or hopeless or crazy. All those labels are irrelevant. What we want to look at is this: what is the past decision behind the present problem?

Often we find the past decision doesn't just affect one specific area in our lives, but actually *is* our whole approach to life. I call choices like these *life decisions* because, after making them, we organize our lives pretty much around those decisions—not just our behavior but our perceptions as well.

For example, if your life decision is to suffer, you'll perceive almost everything that happens to you as a source of suffering—including things other people would see as a source of happiness. If you're praised for a piece of good work, for you that praise will be received as, "Oh, no, now I'm going to have to live up to this standard every time." Sufferers, you see, have the ability to snatch disaster from every victory.

There are many people who, in childhood, make a life decision to be perfect. Others have made the decision to be so agreeable that everyone will love them. Then there are those who want the world to know they are different and that a special set of rules applies to them. And the martyrs whose halos are so tight they give everybody around them a headache. . . . Now, I'm not making fun of these types. I have met countless examples of them all, and they've come to me in very real pain.

The point is, happy people have also made a life decision: to be happy. And this often is not a life decision made in childhood. As you'll see in the following chapters, many—in fact, most—happy people came to that life decision after having operated previously under damaging or at least numbing life decisions like the ones I've just described. Some shocking occurrence or series of circumstances led them to the change in life decision.

III. Find the Context for the Original Decision (Ask Yourself When It Was Made)

When Susan made her original decision about men, her

operative decision, it seemed appropriate if not absolutely necessary. This became clear as I listened to her, not judging: she ensured her mother's love by adopting her position about men. Men were the enemy as far as her mother was concerned, and Susan wasn't about to cast any longing looks toward the enemy camp. So her mother took care of her and kept her safe and approved of her. Her operative decision about men, carried into adult life, brought her not security but problems and disappointments. Susan, of course, was truly unaware of the original decision that kept her from getting what she wanted.

You can see that finding out the context in which you made your original decision can be crucial. I have found that if I really understand the context, no decision is completely stupid or irrational. Often, as in Susan's case, it may have seemed the only viable choice at the time. Even the most bizarre decisions will turn out to have an internal logic.

Let's say a young man refuses, consistently, to do any work. He goes to school but doesn't do any of the assignments. He drops out and gets a job. When someone tells him to do something he says, "Take this job and shove it." He absolutely refuses to do anything with his life.

This is obviously not a functional way of behaving. I try to find out how he came to make the decision not to do whatever was expected or demanded of him. What was the operative decision, yes—but also, what was the context in which it was made?

I discovered that when he was a child, he was eager to do anything that was asked of him—at first. But before long he began to get a very discouraging message: it wasn't good enough, whatever he did. All he got for his efforts was criticism—or, even worse, ridicule from his parents and his older brother and sister. "Look how he sets the table. He's got it all backward. The knife goes on the right, dummy!" And then they would laugh.

On other occasions his efforts were rewarded with anger and

punishment. It wasn't long before he found that whenever he undertook to do something he would stop before he was finished—after all, he'd never be able to do it well enough to satisfy his perfectionist parents. The next step after that was not even to start.

Sensibly enough, *given the context,* he made a life decision: never to attempt anything. If he didn't do anything, he couldn't be criticized or laughed at or punished. Or if he didn't make an effort and they even criticized him for that, he at least would have chosen the censure by not performing in the first place. His ego was then protected from those earlier betrayals of trust that children so often experience. Within the context of his early life, this decision not to do anything seemed rational, even appropriate.

One of the problems in dealing with decisions is finding out which one is operative. Usually there is a whole hierarchy of decisions, and every decision you make influences every future decision. Not only that, but sometimes the important decision—the operative one—stands behind a decision far more easily spotted.

This was the case with Margaret, a woman who asked me for help in carrying through a decision to stop seeing her boyfriend. He was making her miserable with his constant criticism and rudeness; even worse was his habit of playing offensive practical jokes on Margaret and whatever friends or relatives came around.

We didn't have to go very far into Margaret's life to find out why she wasn't able to break up with her obnoxious boyfriend—she didn't know anyone else who could give her such a hard time. Her choice, as it turned out, was to suffer. The boyfriend was only an instrument in carrying out this decision. The decision in front was to stop seeing the boyfriend. The decision behind the decision—the operative one—was whether or not she was going to stop suffering.

IV. List the Payoffs for the Decision

Margaret's original decision to suffer had been made in response to parents who were generally supportive only when she was having problems. Once she could see the advantages of her suffering—the payoffs—she was able to weigh them against the advantages and change her operative decision.

It's enormously helpful to take a look at the payoffs for a decision to suffer, or to act crazy, or to stay depressed. And it's possible to recognize the payoffs even if you can't remember what childhood situation prompted the behavior in the first place.

One depressed patient of mine became very thoughtful when I asked him about possible payoffs. "Well," he said, "my wife doesn't make many demands on me because I'm so depressed. And the kids, they take a look at my face when I get home from work and don't give me a lot of noise or problems." He was quiet for a moment and then went on. "I never thought of it this way before, but on my job they're glad to get the bare minimum from me, so I don't get a lot of pressure from management. Anyone can see I'm depressed, and they sort of write me off." He grinned. "I used to be afraid they'd promote me, and now I don't worry about that anymore."

"That's wonderful," I told him. "Look at what we have to work with. These are real payoffs and now we can weigh them against the payoffs for not being depressed—now you can decide which ones you want. We really don't need your childhood, interesting though it might be."

I never think about payoffs without remembering Irwin, a patient who came to me suffering from a depression so pervasive that it was infecting his whole family. His catalogues of trauma and drama were unrelievedly gloomy and pessimistic. (I always scheduled Irwin late in the afternoon, he affected my own mood so much.) Business was terrible, he was going to have to sell everything, the future was so black that it was hard to see how life was even worth living . . .

I found myself wondering how this woebegone groaner managed to eke out a living selling anything. Yet every once in a while, between lamentations, I would hear that he was buying a new car, that he had just paid his children's expensive tuition bills, that his wife needed another diamond bracelet. "Needed"? "Another"?

"What would happen," I asked him, "if you went out on Forty-Seventh Street tomorrow, smiling and telling everyone business is great?"

Irwin swallowed hard. "That would be the end of me," he said. "Curtains. My credit would dry right up, everybody would be coming around to collect. I'd have to sell everything." It turned out that "selling everything" meant selling a couple of million dollars' worth of diamonds.

"So it's great for business, this depression of yours," I pointed out. "In fact, according to your methods it's absolutely necessary."

We talked about this, and Irwin was finally able to see that a business tactic of long standing had taken over his whole approach to life. His depression wasn't so much a psychological condition as it was a professional uniform.

"Why don't you try something," I suggested. "Go on acting depressed when you're at work, and try to relax [I couldn't bring myself, looking at Irwin, to say be happy] when you're at home. You know, unwind and enjoy yourself a little. After all, it's hard work acting depressed."

Now we could have spent years examining the effects of Irwin's childhood on his adult behavior—how his father-the-salesman acted the same way, or his mother made sure he felt terrible whenever he succeeded at anything. But as an already functional, secretly successful adult, Irwin needed only to become aware of what he was doing before he could decide not to take his depressive act so seriously.

I've used Irwin's story as an example because the payoff in his case is so obvious. But he also illustrates how pervasive anyone's behavior can become, once an operative decision has been made. If you decide to behave in an atypical way, as a response to a perceived or real threat to your survival, you're likely to find this behavior generalizing itself into a life style. In order to do an acting job good enough to convince others, we usually have to convince ourselves first.

A child whose ego is just forming can make a damaging life decision because he feels he is being nullified by constant ridicule and criticism. The boy who refused to do anything was only protecting himself as best he knew how. He would have just as surely curled up into a little ball if the bigger people had him cornered and were raining physical instead of psychic blows upon him. He had no conscious knowledge of why he had started protecting himself this way, and the protective behavior generalized through his life to the point that it became his basic response to the world. He was on automatic pilot until he became aware that the decision to do anything or not was his own.

It's interesting that the same sort of decision, consciously arrived at and applied to a specific situation, can actually solve a problem. Martha is a happy woman I interviewed for this book who on one occasion had deliberately decided not to do anything. Her husband refused to give her enough money to run their household without daily scenes—requests for money from her, demands for explanations and lectures from him. She put up with the situation until she decided that it was intolerable.

Then she made an announcement. Either he would give her a weekly allowance adequate to run the household, or she would stop running the household. He didn't believe her, and so Martha went on strike. She went to bed—and stayed there, reading and listening to music, deaf to her husband's demands that she do anything. He finally gave up. He agreed to the allowance, and Martha resumed her job as homemaker with the dignity of a weekly paycheck.

If Martha's "strike" hadn't produced the desired effect, she would have tried some other way of getting her husband to see things her way. The point is, her do-nothing behavior was undertaken after a conscious decision. It began as a tactic—and was abandoned when she no longer needed it.

V. Examine Your Alternatives to the Behavior That's Causing the Problem

Another woman whose husband treated her the same way Martha's did came to me in very real despair. "What can I do?" she wanted to know. "I love the miserable bastard, but I can't take the way he treats me any longer. I don't know whether to kill him or just kill myself."

I realize that life sometimes seems as hopeless as this, but I assure you it seldom really is. If we paint ourselves into a corner facing the wall, we cut off a lot of perspective. There are always alternatives, though it's often hard to see them when we're stuck in an unhappy situation.

In my practice, I have found that the greatest favor I can do for a patient is to let him discover the answer to the question himself. It's so easy to see another person's alternatives to an unhappy situation. It's tempting to become an evangelist for what, to an outsider, seems like the perfect choice. It's so much better, of course, to give someone the tools to solve his own problem of the moment—plus all those problems that are sure to come up in the future.

What I'm trying to offer in Direct Decision Therapy is a method of dealing with problems in general. I'm not interested in selling you a solution or alternative—I couldn't, even if I wanted to, because I don't know what your options are or even what the specific problem is. I'm interested in helping you see a variety of solutions for a variety of problems.

Once we see that we are not locked into an unhappy situation by anything more than a past decision, the search for present alternatives can be exciting. I remember a call girl who was seeing me because she felt trapped in "the life" to the point of considering suicide. "I hate myself," she said. "I'm just a piece of merchandise. I sell myself."

"So do a lot of people," I pointed out. "Look at lawyers . . ." I was going to continue with a long list, including psychotherapists, but she cut me off.

"That's a good idea. I'm going to become a lawyer."

And she did.

VI. Choose Your Alternative and Decide to Put It into Practice

In choosing an alternative, it's useful to keep in mind the fact that choosing an alternative and making a wish aren't the same thing. Many of us confuse wishes with decisions. When the call girl told me she was going to become a lawyer, she seemed, to me, to be expressing a wish. But once she started to put a plan into action, she was acting on a decision, and I found it easy to take her seriously. And sure enough, four years later she graduated from law school.

I wasn't being sexist in treating her decision, at first, as a wish. I do that with everyone—I don't jump up and start cheering, even if the path to decision has been agonizing for both of us. This is not to say that people shouldn't get encouragement in carrying out their decisions, only that there are more realistic methods of support than cheering. One of the best ways to support somebody's decision is to make him convince you that he is, indeed, committed to it. This gives him the opportunity to consider all the ramifications of the change he's planning to make.

Suppose the problem is drugs. "Why do you want to give it up?" I've asked more than one patient. "After all, with drugs you have a tremendous way of dealing with anxiety." I give him back the reasons he has given me in the past for using drugs. I remind him of how hard it is to kick the drug habit. At this point he has the possibility of making a real—and realistic—choice. He can balance the old payoffs against the anticipated new payoffs and choose.

Sometimes the old payoffs seem too important to make giving up the behavior worthwhile. This is more likely to be the case when the payoff for present behavior is avoiding or reducing anxiety. Warren was a patient who kept his truly intolerable anxiety at bay through not asserting himself. He *never* had the courage to speak up; he was *always* being taken advantage of; he *knew* everyone dismissed him as unimportant. "I'm a wimp," he explained. "An intelligent wimp, but a wimp. And there's no way on earth I'm going to change."

"That's fine," I said. "But can you see that it's your decision not to assert yourself? Let's take a look at the payoffs. What's in it for you?" If we look at the payoffs together, and if he knows I'm not judging him for his decision, it is easier for him to see that this is a choice he probably made long ago, but his choice nonetheless.

Now he is no longer a victim of his nonassertiveness; now he is someone behaving the way he behaves because he has chosen one particular set of payoffs over other possibilities. Warren, having seen himself in this light, decided he didn't even *want* to change. Instead of changing it, he became comfortable with the "wimpy" behavior that had so damaged his view of himself.

This isn't to say that Warren didn't change. He changed from being a nonassertive person who hated himself for letting others take advantage of him to a nonassertive person on whom many others depended. (Which, it turned out, was the way other people had seen Warren all along.) What changed was not his behavior but his experience of it.

I never try to get people to change—I only try to get them to be aware of their choices. If I insist on change, they are right back in the same kind of relationship with authority they've had in the past—which often caused the trouble to begin with. Many of us trace the beginning of our troublesome behavior to the people who tried (for what they honestly believed was our good) to make us behave one way when we wanted to act some other way.

If, on the other hand, *they* decide that a new set of payoffs will make their lives more satisfying, convincing me or a friend or even just themselves can clarify the new decision and open up avenues of action for carrying it out.

Then we can cheer.

VII. Support Yourself in Carrying Out the New Decision

Now when someone has made a decision to change and is truly convinced that the new payoffs will be more rewarding than the old payoffs, the next job is to help him carry through on the decision. Old habits die hard. The euphoria experienced right after the deeision is made may evaporate quickly in the face of automatic, ingrained responses. And the decision itself can evaporate if we don't realize that a slip back into our old behavior doesn't mean we're a failure, or that the decision was a bad decision.

For example, when I decide to lose weight, I can't just decide it once. I have to decide it every time I sit down to eat. The choice is mine, every time: do I want this food? Or do I want to be slim? There I am, faced with the steak and baked potato, the sour cream and chives, the homemade rolls and fresh butter, the salad with real roquefort dressing, the butterscotch praline ice cream—not to mention the cocktail before, the wine during, and the brandy after the meal.

Checking myself out in the mirror, I can see that all too often I decide in favor of the food. The payoff is pretty obvious—I love to eat. But sometimes I decide "enough," and then I decide and decide and decide all day long. Every temptation to eat something fattening means a new decision. But eventually, if I stick with my decision, the weight begins to go.

Since I am familiar with breaking my diet decisions, I know the temptation of saying to myself, "There goes the body beautiful," of feeling guilty for not sticking to my decision and therefore comforting myself with more food. Not only is feeling guilty a clever way to ensure that I will fall off the diet wagon again, but if I feel guilty I don't have to take responsibility for my behavior. That piece of chocolate cake just fell right out of the sky and into my mouth, I really feel terrible about it . . .

The fact is, no one gives a damn when I feel guilty. It just doesn't make one bit of difference. I get fat when I eat too much, so if I'm going to eat too much I might as well enjoy it. And if I stick with my decision to diet, I'll get thin and be able to enjoy *that*.

So I recommend that when you have a lapse from grace, you simply acknowledge it—"I broke my diet," or whatever—and continue carrying out your decision. That's all. No need to agonize or dramatize. The good therapist in us all can remind us that (*a*) the decision has to be made constantly, and (*b*) just because we have slipped, that doesn't mean it's all over—unless we decide it is.

Another way of supporting yourself is to realize you may learn something valuable from the experience of *not* carrying through on a decision. This was the case with Harry, a man I had been seeing who made a decision to stop drinking. He got support for this decision and succeeded in staying sober for months. Then, one night, he got drunk. But when he got drunk this time, Harry knew that getting drunk was *his* decision. He didn't say, "I don't know what came over me." He knew perfectly well what had come over him, and he wanted to take a look at the context for his decision to get drunk—and at the payoffs.

He had been out with a beautiful woman that night, and Harry realized that he got drunk only when he was out with a beautiful woman. "All the guys at the bar were smiling at her," he said, "and every time I tried to say anything, all I could think of was that she'd rather be with one of them. They seemed so relaxed, and I was so nervous—before long I had convinced myself that she'd leave me on my barstool and go off. So instead of sticking to my decision not to drink, I ordered a drink. Of course, I kept on drinking and feeling less anxious but also getting drunk. So she left me on my barstool and went off!"

It seemed to me that Harry got a great deal more insight into what triggered his problem drinking from examining why he chose not to stick to his decision than could have been achieved in quite a few sessions of traditional therapy.

3

Step I: Decide What You Want in Order to Be Happy (or Happier)

CECELIA was a black, middle-aged clerk in a toy department where I found myself looking for presents for my grandchildren. I was struck by her intense involvement in helping me find just the right toy for each child. She not only asked me questions, she listened to the answers as I became grandfatherly in telling her how unusual my little friends were. She wasn't trying to sell me anything, she was just having so much fun demonstrating each toy that I found myself reluctant to leave her company.

I told her that I was interviewing happy people for a book and that she struck me as a very happy person. I was delighted when she agreed to meet me for lunch—and she was enormously pleased that I thought her interesting enough to include in a book. Unlike most people who have been made self-conscious by a compliment, Cecelia became visibly more open and composed with each answer to a question. She had what I think of as a "queenly" sense of self—she seemed to dignify everything around her with her nobility of spirit.

Her life had been anything but privileged. She had grown up in a ghetto, raised by parents who were loving but always working to support the family at the barest subsistence level. She had been married quite young to an alcoholic who deserted her after terrorizing her for a few years with increasingly violent bouts of drunkenness. Not long after that, her father, to whom she was very close, died.

"I was real sad for a long time. But you know, when I thought about what a wonderful man he had been and how much he loved me, I decided my father would want me to be the way he loved me—cheerful and enjoying myself. He always said I could light up the room, we didn't need electricity."

As for her husband, Cecilia quickly realized how much better off she was without him. The marriage could only have gotten even worse as his alcoholism progressed. She told me that his desertion had actually lifted a weight off her shoulders: she could stop being afraid in her own house.

"Yes, sir, I'm fifty-six years old now and I've got no man. You know, my friends and family keep on saying, 'You poor old thing,' and they can't believe it when I laugh and say, 'Don't you feel sorry for me.' Poor old *me*?" Her laughter rang out, rich and musical. "What good is that kind of thinking going to do me? What will it buy me?"

"I was miserable with that man around. I've got all kinds of freedom now, and I'd rather have it than a man any day. I go to the movies when I want, I have my friends over, I can stay up all night and sleep all day on the weekends and watch television twenty-four hours if I want. I do what pleases *me,* and I please to have some fun in my life."

Cecelia's ability to redefine a situation had been characteristic of her from the start. She was an adopted child whose mother had left her with an agency and disappeared. "I was abandoned" is the way a lot of people see it, sometimes setting themselves up as victims from the very beginning. Not Cecelia. "My parents chose me personally," she said with pride.

But Cecelia's most important attribute, it seemed to me, was that she didn't take herself or her troubles very seriously. She found humor in every one of the circumstances she described. She was the kind of person who always produces a laugh in her listener—and her own laugh was the sort that makes you smile even before you know what the joke is.

Not only is laughter therapeutic (especially when you are in a quandary), but laughter and depression are genuinely incompatible. Laughter *literally* makes you feel good: it releases chemicals in the brain akin to amphetamines and cocaine.

Our world tends to open up whenever we stop taking everything so seriously. Unexpected solutions present themselves without much effort on our part. Suddenly we know what we feel like doing. And as Cecelia well knows, under those circumstances even hard work can be fun.

Camus, in *The Myth of Sisyphus,* wrote that a person who has not contemplated suicide and eventually rejected the idea has not really decided to live.

This is the basic decision. There's one situation that makes therapy impossible: when the patient has never decided to live. I don't mean "exist"—tiptoeing or sleepwalking through life. I mean making a conscious decision to live. Once this happens, therapy is easy.

There is often a very good reason why a patient may never have confronted this question. If he has grown up with indications that his parents never wanted him, he may feel guilty for being alive—so he apologizes for it. You know the expression, "Pardon me for living." One of the first questions I ask such a patient is, "How about it? What do you want? To live or die?"

It's interesting that a common thread running through the lives of quite a few happy people I interviewed was a literal brush with death. Contemplating the significance of life and death wasn't a philosophical matter for them. It was an experience that allowed them to perceive life as a gift. Having been confronted with how problem-free death is, they then could see their daily problems as opportunities for feeling alive.

Carl was a retired army master sergeant I met when he joined one of my psychology classes. He had boundless curiosity about everything and threw himself into whatever activity was at hand with full concentration. His pleasure was infectious, whether he was repairing a broken light fixture or participating in my class. It felt good just to be around Carl; and without even asking, all your broken light fixtures got repaired.

When I asked him if he'd always been so happy, he said, "Not exactly. I can tell you when and how it happened. When I first joined the army, I was out waterskiing one day and took a freak fall. It paralyzed me, and I started to drown. You know how you drown? You don't get water in your lungs, you swallow so much water that you sink."

He was picked out of the water at the last minute and rushed to a hospital. The doctor who examined him said, "You're a very serious case. You may not make it, and if you do make it there's a good chance you'll be paralyzed for life."

Carl, undismayed by the doctor's bedside manner, said firmly, "I'm going to get better." And he did. After many months in the hospital, he walked out. "I remember the blueness of the sky and the greenness of the grass. I had this lightheaded feeling of being on borrowed time, and I remember saying, out loud, 'I'm going to have a *good* time.'"

Carl's good time consisted of doing the things he loved to do—fixing anything broken, taking courses to satisfy his curiosity, helping people out, lovingly restoring an ancient Cadillac for himself. His family caught his spirit and helped each other, working together, enjoying each other. Family life, as Carl described it, was "corny and very pleasant."

I still wanted to know how happy he had been before his accident. Not very, it turned out. He had grown up in the Chicago slums, in an overcrowded apartment with a father who beat him and a mother who was shrewish and possessive. She never let him alone, and nothing he did escaped her critical eye. Carl joined the army and got away from this oppression.

But until his accident, he realized, he had been drifting through his assignments, "out of focus. I can't say I was actively happy, just passively appreciating the absence of chaos that always surrounded me at home."

Now Carl had done something that a lot of happy people are able to do. He'd had the good sense to renounce apparent success for a life style that he found more satisfying. After a few years in the army, he impressed his superior officers so much that he was given a commission. The trouble was, he discovered he didn't enjoy the company of officers. And he felt the pressure of career politics not worth his attention. Once he realized he had liked enlisted life better, he resigned his commission for his old rank. He never regretted the decision.

Carl and Cecelia illustrate a very important prerequisite for happiness. They have the capacity to make decisions based on what *they* want—not what their family, friends, or coworkers want for them.

"What do you want?" "What would make you happy?"
These are the first questions to ask yourself if you want to use Direct Decision Therapy. "Not a man, no sir," said Cecelia. "Not a commission, I'm happy where I was," said Carl. The majority of people would probably disagree with their decisions, but both Carl and Cecelia knew what choice was right for them.

Pamela is a pretty young woman I knew when I lived in New York. I saw her from time to time, and she usually seemed discontented. Then one summer I ran into her and she was so obviously happy I thought she must have fallen in love. No, I found out, it wasn't love, it was a summer house in the Hamptons she'd just rented a part of. "I don't have to stay in this sweltering, sweaty city this summer," she said. "I'm going to have a wonderful time."

On the hottest weekend in July, I was surprised to see Pamela again. "Why aren't you in the Hamptons?" I asked her.

"It's a long story," she said, "but the bottom line is that I spent $2,000 to find out I love being in New York. I never realized it until I started commuting to Southampton and missed all the things there are to do here, all the options, all my friends. Probably the best $2,000 I ever spent—better than air conditioning. Think I've flipped?"

She wasn't a patient, and I don't know how she switched her discontent for her obvious state of satisfaction. I liked her reasoning, and it was a pleasure to see how happy her decision made her—even in that heat.

What do you really want? What would make you happy? In answering the question many people will say, "I want so-and-so but I can't have it." Or, "Whatever I want, I can't have." Or even, "I want *whatever* I can't have." (As one female patient of mine put it, "It seems as though the most appealing characteristic a man can have for me is unavailability.")

Most of us become convinced at some point in our lives that what we want the most, right then, is something we absolutely can't have. Very often it's a person, but it can also be something we can't afford, literally or figuratively. In many cases we can become a lot happier simply by reordering our experience, which is what Pamela did. For example, instead of saying, "I want a man and then I'll be happy," you might say, "I want to be happy even though I don't have a man, *and* I also want a man." The fact is, you have a far better chance of attracting a member of the opposite sex when you're happy with your life than when you're discontented and looking for a relationship.

One of our problems with happiness may be that in the past

when we *did* obtain or achieve something we were sure would make us happy, it disappeared—or it didn't make any difference after a while. Dissatisfaction returned. The sky wasn't bluer and the sun didn't shine any brighter. We were still trying to get happiness from outside ourselves.

A lover leaves, a car is wrecked, a job is lost, a house is burned— losses like these can knock the wind out of us. One difference between basically happy people and others is that the happy person's recovery time is shorter. When you think about it, you can't be really happy if you can't be really sad. But happy people have a sense that whatever happens, things will eventually work out. In short, they trust themselves to react in their own best interest.

By best interest I don't mean narrow self-interest. The happy people I've known have a fine awareness of how they are related to the world. Of how like each other we are and—even more important—how we differ from others, where we leave off and another person begins. A happy person's best interest includes concern for others; when it comes to himself, he is comfortable with his uniqueness and able to nurture it.

I drove by a nursery school not long ago and watched children bursting through the doors like corks out of champagne bottles. There were so exuberant, so manic, so wild. They ran around shrieking and laughing, tumbling and literally jumping for joy.

After thirty years of listening to people free their sense of self from all the fences put around it by parents, teachers, and society, I am likely to be reminded every time I see unsupervised children that a sense of self is something we all have before the fences hem us in. Children are naturally happy, even manic.

Society doesn't want you to be that way; your parents can't stand it either. Sooner or later that kind of spontaneity has to be controlled if the child is going to be able to get along in the world.

But this is how children are, naturally, when they aren't controlled. No one has to tell them how to be happy.

If you watch them at play, it's so obvious that children also have a natural sense of humor. They're always doing or saying funny things. It's not just that we find them amusing; they find what they do (and the world they do it in) funny. And this gets trained out of them.

We'll punish them because they'll be funny at inappropriate times or in an inappropriate place (such as church), or we'll say "time to get serious" as if we mean "time to get normal," the way people are supposed to be. So eventually the humor may get trained out of them along with the manic joy.

I'm not saying that it's tragic or awful that children have all these things trained out of them. It's just that so many of us lose touch with these capabilities when we grow up. We *need* some training in order to grow up. And there are times, certainly, when it would be inappropriate to be funny. The important thing is not to be compulsive in either direction. There are so many times when the response of laughter, or of humor in some form, is wonderfully constructive and appropriate.

It's so hard for us to give up taking ourselves seriously. But a sense of humor can be recaptured. I've seen it happen—one of the surest signs that a patient is getting better is when he begins to be able to see what's funny about himself and his life. A sense of the absurd can go such a long way in counteracting the heavy dramatizations that we engage in so much of the time.

"A sense of humor is a fine thing," a man said to me not long ago. "I just wish I had one." It doesn't help much to tell a person he started out with a sense of humor as a child if he feels he's lost it as an adult. When asked "What do you want? What would make you happy?" quite a few people will say something like, "I want to enjoy myself more, I'd like to be able to laugh at things. I'd like not to be so grim."

The first thing to remember is that there are two kinds of humor: creative and receptive. This is important—without an audience, it's very hard to be funny. Sometimes when I use examples while speaking on the subject of humor in therapy, the audience roars. Other times they don't respond, and then I find it impossible to be very funny at all. My cousin owned a resort in the Catskills, and I considered becoming a comedian until I thought: "Hey, if they don't laugh, I'm dead." (So now I'm a therapist, and if they don't laugh I can just get serious.)

The point is that the consumer of humor is just as important as the creator. You're very fortunate if you have both kinds of humor, if you can both create and appreciate it. But the appreciating is something we can all do.

This is why I sometimes say to a person who thinks he doesn't have a sense of humor: if you think you don't have it, that means you already recognize that other people do have it. Which means you do have one type, the receptive capability. The best thing you can do is to be aware of this capability and let yourself give the gift of laughter to the person or situation that's funny. Let yourself (notice I don't say "make" yourself) enjoy other people's humor. The very decision to let yourself laugh can accomplish a lot in this area.

It's interesting that the comedian and the therapist both deal in material that's not normally mentioned in polite society. It's such a relief from the tension of holding this hot (or heavy) stuff in, and so we laugh. And laughter, long thought to be a tension reliever, is now known to trigger the release in our brains of endorphins—substances that create a feeling of well-being. Like those nursery school kids racing around on joy mania, we can produce our own natural highs.

Neurochemists have discovered receptors in our brains for all the mood-altering drugs available. This means that our bodies also must have the ability to produce the analogs of these drugs. So those children really were high, they were speeding—the little junkies. Why can't we send ourselves on our own euphoric trips? The research now being done on brain chemistry suggests that we can.

I won't be surprised when they find out just how we can do it. Before anyone knew that endorphins or any other druglike natural chemicals existed in our brains, I had experienced some success in simulating a drug trip for addicted patients. One woman, who claimed she always felt high on marijuana after hypnosis, sent friends who wanted to kick the pot habit to be taught how to hypnotize themselves so they could get by without the weed.

I also had success with simulated LSD therapy—but only, I noticed, among patients who had decided beforehand that the therapy was going to succeed.

My most notable accomplishment in the area of hypnosis and drugs was with a heroin addict named Gladys who had tried (and failed) to kick the habit with every method she'd ever heard of. Gladys and I worked out a method together. She showed me exactly how she gave herself a fix, step by step, using her finger as the needle. I then hypnotized her and proceeded to suggest, step by step, that she was giving herself a fix. As she went through the motions, she would get high.

When she came out of the trance, Gladys said, "That was great stuff you laid on me." She felt wonderful—even though she should have been going through withdrawal, not having had a fix since the day before. I then hypnotized her again and suggested that whenever she wanted a fix, she would say to herself the number 263 and put her fingertip to her arm just as if it were her "spike" (the hypodermic needle). The minute her finger touched her arm, I suggested, she would feel high.

Now when Gladys first came to me I was surprised and flattered at her insisting I was the only therapist in New York who could treat her. It was only after several weeks that I understood the reason—her source of heroin was around the corner from my office, and she was playing it safe. Nevertheless, in a short time she learned how to carry out the suggestion—or, as she called it, the mental fix—by herself, with great success.

Her addict friends would invite her to join them in shooting up, and she surprised herself by being able to turn down the opportunity. Then, one afternoon, they got to her. Gladys's usual habit was two "nickel bags"—two glassine envelopes of heroin at $5 apiece (old prices, this is an old story). Gladys decided to save money and used only half a bag along with, at the same time, a mental fix. Several hours later she woke from an overdose reaction.

If those researchers are right, then the hypnotic suggestion really did produce the analog of heroin in her brain, and that, combined with the half bag, was too much for Gladys. Anyway, she never did the real stuff again. When last I heard from her, some of her junkie friends were offering $25 for the magic number.

I think Gladys kicked the habit because she made a decision to kick the habit, not because I hypnotized her. The hypnotic suggestion simply enabled her to do it more comfortably—the suggestion, along with those great natural drugs in her brain, that is.

Psychotherapists often describe the addiction of people who abuse alcohol or other drugs as connected to a desire to return to the happy euphoria of childhood. Searching for the Garden of Eden of infancy—that land of milk and honey where all our needs were met, where we never had to work, where everything was taken care of as long as we didn't make the mistake of getting too intelligent by eating the apple of knowledge.

But of course we did eat the apple, we blew it. So what do we do now? One of the things we as adults have going for us is that, unlike children, we have enough experience to be able to see the connection between actions and results. We can make choices with a good chance of seeing how they will affect our future.

Choosing to be happy is a way of awakening that trust in our instincts that was so characteristic of us as children. Happy grownups, I've discovered, either never lost that ability or have developed it as they learned from their adult experience.

Choosing to reclaim our control over the great powers our brains are capable of is one way of asserting our independence from all the exterior circumstances seeking to control *us*. Perhaps we may have the apple of knowledge and recapture our childlike delight, too.

"What do you want?" *I want to be happy*. And why not? The thing is, if you're going to exist, you might as well decide to live. And as long as you're deciding to live, you might as well decide to be happy.

It doesn't occur to most people that they can make such a choice—"Maybe I can decide to be a little bit happy, or happier, but HAPPY?" I think it depends on the priorities you set for yourself. Listen to this: "I want to be happy but I am anxious all the time." Did it ever occur to you that you could be a happy anxious person?

Here's another thing I've observed. Wanting to know *how* to be happy before *choosing* to be happy is definitely doing it the hard way. First, decide to be happy. Notice I didn't say "be happy," just decide to be. "The hell with all this grim business, I want to be happy." Believe me, right away the problems in your life will not seem so overwhelming. It will be a lot easier to figure out what to do about them, too. If you know where you're headed, you allow yourself to be responsible for getting there.

We're all interested in such fancy, complicated ways of dealing with our problems, when often the simplest way—turning them into opportunities—will work better. If you can turn problems into opportunities, then you will be happy to hear that the solutions to our present problems contain the seeds of our future problems.

Think about that. And about this, too: when you've reached the point in your life where you don't have problems, you've reached the end of your life. You're dead.

So why be so grim about life? Because there are such serious problems, personal and global? But some things are so serious that they are best treated with humor. The best thing ever done about nuclear holocaust, for my money, was *Dr. Strangelove: Or How I Learned to Stop Worrying and Love the Bomb*. Finding what is ludicrous, ridiculous, absurd in our lives is finding our capacity for happiness.

Enough of convincing you that happier is easier and makes grass and cocaine obsolete. Sometimes I won't let myself appreciate results unless I have proved I deserve them with sweating and agonizing. The rewards-equal-effort ethic is hard to banish.

Maybe you want to wait and see—not commit yourself to being a happy person until one unmanageable problem in your life is cleared up. Direct Decision Therapy can work on the installment plan, too. If you learn to follow the steps, you are going to become aware of your choices and get some practice in deciding which ones you want to guide your life and which ones you want to change.

I don't think people *should* be happy. I only think life is more satisfying if we are aware of what we are choosing. If your choice is to be sad, or to suffer, that's fine with me. I happen to know some very interesting morose people who are just as valuable as happy people. In the case of some of them, their moroseness can make me happy. Remember Oscar Levant? If he had been exuding happiness, he would have made his fans very disappointed. Some people, myself included, find it more fun to be happy—and that's what this book is about.

So you can give the question, "What do I want?" the answer, "I want to be happy." (Even if you don't know if you *can* be happy.) What problems or deficiencies in your life are preventing you from feeling happy? More important, what do you want to do about them?

You may have an external or internal goal. "I want to get a better-paying job that will be satisfying" is an example of an external goal. "I want to be less anxious" is an example of an internal goal.

Now deciding what you want doesn't have to be a major decision. If you're intimidated when it comes to big decisions, start with tiny ones—"I am going to eat an ice cream cone," or "I am never going to eat spinach again." (Clarence Darrow said, "I hate spinach and I'm glad I do, because if I liked it I'd eat it and I just hate it.")

In making a conscious choice about how things are going to be in your life, your course can be charted by just such a series of small steps—tiny progressions toward becoming a happy person. If you draw a blank at first, I've added a sort of incentive checklist below to get you started. It's not a test—there aren't even any questions, just leading statements—so going down the list can be an optional, totally nonthreatening, and enjoyable experience.

Succeeding chapters will also have incentive checklists, with space after each in case you choose to add your own. But starting now, with Step I, you can relax and enjoy this journey. I hope you can have fun—just like a kid—reading about happy alternatives. At the least, maybe something on the list will make you laugh and trigger the release of an endorphin.

Step I: What Do You Want in Order to Be Happy (or Happier)?

- Think of the first five things that come to your mind when you say "I want to be happy."

- Think of something you want right now.

- Think of something you want right now, and figure out how you might get it.

- Lay out clothes for tomorrow that make *you* feel comfortable, not the designer.

- Decide not to start an argument—unless you enjoy it.

- Decide to smile a lot tomorrow morning, and see what happens.

- Do something physical enough to work up a sweat.

- Go to an airport, and pretend you're leaving.

- Decide to take ten seconds the next time you're angry, and use them to put yourself in the other person's place.

- Consider this: usually what makes you angry is your belief that somebody or something shouldn't be the way it is.

- Decide to finish something today that could easily wait until tomorrow.

- Decide to put off till tomorrow something that could easily be finished today.

- Think of a friend you've been meaning to get in touch with, and call him.

- Think of a friend you've been meaning to get in touch with, and decide not to get in touch.

- Go to a fancy department store and try on makeup.

- Figure out something you do that is above criticism, and decide to do it more often.

- Do some research about something you've always disliked, and see if you still dislike it so much.

- Take inventory of the little things that upset you almost every day, and try to see the humor in them.

- Try something radical: open all your mail and return every phone call.

- Try something radical: put all your mail aside for six months, and see if it really makes any difference.

- Figure out your happiest activities, and imagine who you'd like to do them with.

- Figure out your happiest activities, and imagine having fun doing them all by yourself.

• Decide to do something nice for somebody else tomorrow—and not tell anybody you did it.

4

Step II: Find the Decision Behind the Problem

$\mathbb{P}$AUL was a cool number. He had a way of sitting in the group and seeming to be apart from it at the same time. It wasn't that he didn't listen; he was obviously paying close attention to what was going on. It's just that there was no way of telling from his eyes (which looked straight at you when you were talking) what he was thinking or feeling. Everything went in and nothing came out.

His wife, Paul told the group, complained that he drove her crazy and taunted him for not expressing any opinions or preferences about what to do. He claimed matter-of-factly that it didn't matter one way or another to him. He really was willing to do anything she wanted, let her decide since she had stronger feelings about things than he did. Paul referred to his wife with obvious affection, though she did come across (in his unbiased account) as a little bit crazy, a little difficult and demanding. He never made that kind of judgment about Alice; he just seemed perplexed that she wasn't happier with him.

The group enjoyed Paul's disarming descriptions and his dry way of poking fun at himself as a sort of henpecked husband who couldn't seem to please his wife. They all seemed charmed by this low-key, pleasant fellow who was obviously so much more mature than his wife—all except Gwen. I asked her what she thought about Paul's problems with Alice.

"I could kill him," Gwen said. "He would drive me nuts, too. I bet he says 'anything-you-want-dear' and then does exactly what *he* wants to do—because he obviously knows and cares, he's just not telling." She paused for breath and glared at Paul. "I'll bet you don't join her in anything she wants you to, I bet you hide behind the newspaper, extra work from the office, anything that keeps you from sharing. I know you, Paul—because I was married to you for fifteen years. Only the name is different."

Paul listened attentively, his response almost imperceptible. He nodded and arranged his face in a more thoughtful expression. He raised not a word in his own defense. Gwen pointed at him and said, "See? No reaction. What can make you feel crazier than that?"

If Paul hadn't been married to Alice, Gwen would have done nicely. Men like him (we call them passive-aggressives) usually marry dynamic, highly emotional women. Once the honeymoon is over, they proceed to make each other miserable by trying to change each other—one actively, the other passively.

Paul, so charming and superior in his noninvolvement, eventually admitted that he conducted himself along these lines in all areas of his life. He was a stockbroker who never had to sell; he offered reliable information (impartially, of course), and the investor sold himself. Paul's method worked beautifully: he never judged or got involved, and his clients trusted him.

He also admitted that he knew exactly what behavior could set Alice off on a war dance. If she had done something to make him angry, he could release his own charge without lifting a finger—in fact, this was guaranteed to result in an explosion. Alice's fuse was very short from years of slow burns.

I asked Paul if he had always been such a cool character, and he told me that as a child he had been full of daring and enthusiasm, a natural leader making decisions and taking risks for half the boys on the block. When a new boy moved to the neighborhood and began challenging him, Paul—very sure of himself, very well liked—ignored his provocations. Then, one day, the boy attacked him. "I don't really know what happened after that. The next thing I remember was people pulling at me and screaming, and I realized I was beating his head against the sidewalk. I could have killed him. And I decided right then, 'Never again.'"

Paul's *life decision* was to stay cool and never to show anger directly. He felt anger, of course—we all do—but he never expressed it. People who never express anger can enrage other people. Alice knows.

Paul *operational decision* was always to keep a certain distance, never becoming involved beyond the depth of his pleasant and controllable emotions. He became the observer, the amusing reconteur of other people's exploits, the reliable interpreter of data for other people to get excited about. He quite sincerely felt his way to be superior, and in fact it had worked well for him in his life.

Unfortunately for Paul, marriage has a way of peeling away our adult facades and revealing childhood emotions—whether we want it to or not. The more Alice stirred up his anger, the more he needed to find a superior way to handle it. His "solution" was ingenious but not uncommon: his intense, volatile wife acted it out for both of them.

Now, marriage anger once stirred up can assume a life of its own—because so often it has little to do with our spouses, but lots to do with those absent others from our childhood.

Paul came to my therapy group because Alice had said, "Either you go there or I go to a lawyer." She couldn't stand being angry all the time, and she had too strong a sense of self to assume the whole problem was of her making. She also had no "anger" problem with her many friends. What all this added up to for Paul was dissatisfaction with his operational decision. He loved Alice. She was spontaneous, enthusiastic, and—when she wasn't dancing around in fury at Paul—delightful company. She quite possibly reminded

Paul a little of his adventuresome self before he "nearly killed" the new boy on the block.

Were it not for Gwen's outburst, the group might well have reinforced Paul's unspoken judgment that Alice was just too demanding and suggested that he see a lawyer, too. As it was, Paul had the courage to see that passivity can damage as deeply as a bludgeon. He made a real contribution to the group by finding the risk-taking little boy he once had been. As he let the group see more and more of him, he experienced a lot of genuine warmth and acceptance. After all, fear of murderous rage is an emotion most of us can identify with.

I met an old friend not long ago whom I hadn't seen for years. She was a gentle, dreamy woman who always wore a wistful smile. I asked her how she was, and she told me she had gotten married and moved to a pretty house with a garden she loved. Her husband was retired, so they worked in the garden and enjoyed each other's company when she wasn't at her job. He was, she assured me, a wonderful man, and she herself was very happy.

I was happy for her, and said so—but her smile was more wistful than ever. As we started to go our separate ways, she turned and said, "Yes, everything really is fine . . . except for the music."

"What about the music?" She then told me that about once a week her husband would go on a drinking binge and come home to play the "1812 Overture" turned up at top volume all night long. Other than that, her life was fine.

Paul's life really was fine, too—except for the anger. The point is, these "excepts" have a way of getting turned up louder and louder in our lives until we have to listen to them. And the good listener has a far better chance of finding his operative decision and changing it to get rid of his "excepts."

I had a depressed patient once who came to me for analysis. The first five sessions he lay on the couch without saying a word. Ten minutes into the sixth session I finally asked, "Is there anything you'd like to say?" He seemed surprised and said, "I didn't know I was supposed to talk." He then proceeded to say quite a lot, and we continued in the usual way until he completed his analysis. Near the end of the last session, I asked him what he had found most helpful in ending his depression.

"Having somebody there who would listen to me," he said. "Having a reason to look at myself, a time and place where I could really look at what I was doing—why, how, and all of that. But the most helpful time of all was those first five sessions when I didn't say anything. I really went very far inside myself and saw things I'd never allowed myself to see before."

I think that if people could begin to see depression as an opportunity to go into themselves and look at what's there, find parts of themselves they have lost, then depression wouldn't have so much dread attached to it. Instead of always seeing it as a block to happiness, we might start looking at it as a possible path to happiness.

Depression can also be valuable—especially for highly energetic people, the ones who are always involved up to their ears in something or other. Sometimes the only time these people slow down is when they go into a depression. Depression creates a resting space.

Isaac Newton discovered the basic laws of motion after a severe depression. Many writers and painters think they're suffering a paralyzing depression when they are only outwardly inactive, gathering creative forces for a great leap forward.

In my own profession I've come to recognize that in therapy a period always comes in which everything seems to grind to a halt. The patient feels hopeless, and I feel helpless. I know enough now to wait these periods out—and I'm not a patient man—because I've seen how often it ends with a real breakthrough. The patient comes up with a crucial insight for change that is far more profound than any of my infinite wisdom.

Sometimes in order to experience happiness we have to allow ourselves to be unhappy first.

In the years I've been practicing Direct Decision Therapy, depressed patients are the ones who've had the hardest time finding their operative decision. When I ask them (or they ask themselves) what might be the decision behind the depression they're experiencing, they have trouble deciding how to answer the question. After all, a common symptom of depression is the inability to make decisions. Even recognizing a decision already made can be harder when you're depressed.

When the answer is given, it's more likely to come out as "I know I *should*" than as "I decided." Here's how it goes: "I know I should be writing a book and I'm depressed because I'm not." You're helpless there, all right. How can you write a book when you're depressed? So stay depressed and you'll never have to face the anxiety of writing a book. What about, "I decided to avoid the anxiety of writing a book by becoming depressed." That's too easy, right?

Nobody's happy who is operating under "shoulds," and we intensify their oppressive power whenever we make unreasonable demands upon ourselves. Now I find it easy to spot other people's unreasonable demands and yet the ones I make on myself are sometimes anything but reasonable. So many of us say, "Take it easy" to our friends and then turn around and say to ourselves, "In my case the demands are not unreasonable. I should be able to meet them."

In my case, I'm the president of a professional school, I have a private practice, I teach, I lecture all over the world, I paint, I write books—I do all those things and can still consider myself lazy because I don't do as much as I could. This, in fact, is my biggest problem—that I always feel I could be doing more. Of course I could be doing more. Anybody could always be doing more.

Fortunately, I'm onto myself. I hear my hanging judge telling me all the things I should be doing, and I go out and enjoy a long lunch with interesting companions, or go swimming, or do something just for the hell of it. I don't have any trouble getting myself to do what I'm supposed to do, you see. The problem comes when I have fun. That's when I can get should-bound: I'm having a good time, I should be writing; I'm painting a picture, I should be . . . whatever.

That of course is one of the problems many people have. I could be doing so many different things. I have so many choices, too many choices.

Even within my field, I could have focused on one of the many things I do with patients—Direct Decision Therapy, or hypnotherapy, or pure cognitive behavioral therapy—and maybe become famous for it, "realizing my potential" in mental health. But I enjoy taking different approaches at different times and with different patients. The payoff of more prestige or more fame isn't nearly as important as the payoff of enjoying my work. Of trying new approaches with patients, going down untraveled roads.

I could never be happy as a traditional psychoanalyst, sitting behind my desk saying "hmmm . . ." and then, in one of my more creative moments, saying "Hah!" If I tried to fit myself into the classic mold of the psychoanalyst I would make myself very depressed.

Very often, people say they're depressed because they have this terrific potential and they're not living up to it. In one sense they're right, because none of us live up to our potential. What creates the depression is the demand that all that potential be lived up to—the "should."

It seems characteristic of the age we live in that so many of us are so sure we're doing something terrible to ourselves by not living up to our potential. And sometimes we even judge how well we've lived up to it by how much we've suffered. I had a very bright patient who pulled off academic accomplishment after accomplishment while raising four children—and who came to me because she felt convinced she was a fake. Why? "Because it was so easy."

I offer you the same advice I offer myself: Don't live up to your potential. You can't, for one thing. For another, your hanging judge will ensure that your potential always lies beyond any point that you can reasonably reach in the road.

We're all happier, certainly, when we can see that living is challenge enough in itself. I'll never forget a wonderful taxi driver in New York who said, when another car cut him off, "Where's he rushing? To the cemetery, that's where. Now me, I figure that when I get up in the morning, I'm ahead. Anything after that is extra."

Like the taxi driver, I think people who get up in the morning are courageous and worthwhile. There you are, courageous and worthwhile already, standing beside your bed. Now anything more you do all day long is extra, whipped cream, frosting on the cake. So maybe you could choose to enjoy what you do now—you don't have to prove anything.

Maybe you're too angry to enjoy anything. Many depressed people are sitting on a pressure cooker of anger—being angry *is* depressing, because so often there just doesn't seem to be any safe place to put it. It's like a dangerous explosive. And if we follow the modern dictate to "let out" the anger, we often find that letting out our anger just generates more anger.

When you consider that we have been ingesting anger all our lives, it's no wonder there sometimes isn't any appropriate direct release for it. The problem is that the immediate anger stirs up the volcano of anger beneath the surface. And anger short-circuits our thinking processes so that we have panic responses, can't think of choices—unless, like Paul, we have already made a life decision never to express anger directly. And many of us share his operational decision to manipulate (unconsciously) other people into expressing our own anger.

In chapter 8 I'll discuss ways in which an operational decision like Paul's can be changed. For now, I'd like to tell you about an experiment, conducted by one of my students, that suggests an *enjoyable* way of defusing anger.

Two groups of people were deliberately incited to anger, made very angry. One group was given the opportunity to ventilate the anger; the other group was taken to another room where they listened to a talented comedian tell funny jokes. In the two groups, the people who had laughed for an hour felt much better afterward than the people who had "gotten their anger out." Scientists are, in fact, finding that the therapeutic value of laughter isn't just in our minds: laughter releases endorphins, those marvelous brain chemicals capable of calming and healing us.

Anger, too, can be mobilized to heal. On one occasion I asked a patient who was enraged by his medical diagnosis—cancer—to gather all his helpless anger into a laser beam and focus the beam on the site of his cancer. A powerful man, he was able to use his anger in that way to (apparently) obliterate the cancer. Whether this was a cure or not, it certainly relieved his feelings of helplessness.

Many obese patients are angry. In treating them I am sometimes able to direct their anger against the junk food industry, television commercials, the lobbies that manipulate the public to eat, eat, eat. Get mad, don't buy their line, don't be their pawn, they don't care if you eat yourself into an early grave. Even those patients who are punishing their parents or families by staying fat can use their anger to stop punishing themselves. So your parents don't want you to eat, or your family does want you to eat—that's no reason to eat. Maybe you're both in a conspiracy to punish *you*. Show them, take care of yourself.

The most unusual therapeutic use of anger I ever witnessed was on the part of an exhibitionist. This man, a brilliant research scientist and professor, risked a great deal when he exposed himself, though he did travel long distances in order to protect his position.

He was refused tenure by his university shortly after we began therapy. He worked himself into such a rage that he traveled to the nearest large city and exposed himself five times. His *modus operandi* was to stand in front of a store window on a street that wasn't too crowded, knock at the plate glass window until one of the female clerks looked out, and then expose himself.

Like most exhibitionists, he felt better after shocking someone by his outrageous behavior. He told me he was angry at the Establishment, that as a radical he detested the hypocrisy and rigidity of society in general and his professional colleagues in particular. He saw his exhibitionism as a means of showing his contempt for our hypocritical society.

I pointed out that in the very moment he was attacking the Establishment he was actually just playing their game. They believe all radicals are Commie sexual perverts anyway. By thumbing his "whatever" at the Establishment, he was giving them ammunition, confirming them in their opinion of the weird radicals.

Horrified—and convinced—by this line of reasoning, he said, "That's it, I've decided. No more. By God, I'm not going to prove them right."

He really did go "cold turkey." He also began releasing his anger by writing irate letters to newspapers and magazines with such a flair that they often got printed. This constituted such positive feedback that the psuedoassertion of exhibitionism paled in comparison.

In addition to its therapeutic value, anger can be a great motivator. Living well really is the best revenge. And anger can propel us out of passivity into action. Probably the single best setup for depression is the totally impossible demand that we shouldn't get angry. Instead of getting angry (then depressed) about this psychological fact of life, we might change the way we view anger. Anger can be refreshing, anger can be used constructively, anger can be healing—it's only when it's the total response to life that it's debilitating and exhausting.

Anger or depression, it's all a function of the hanging judge. He sits inside us and judges everybody, everything, inside and out. What a creep! (See? He even got me to judge *him*.) So who cares? Throw him out. Judging never solved a problem. Society makes the judgment that we need a judicial system, and we have overflowing prisons to prove it. I don't know the answer, I just know that in therapy—self-help or professionally directed—judging never helps.

If you want to be a good therapist to yourself, stop the judging and recognize that conquering yourself is an impossible task. You'll never be able to substitute a constructive operational decision for a self-defeating one by engaging in a power struggle.

One of the ways I help people reverse self-defeating decisions is by what I call "joining the resistance." It seems to me that most people underestimate the value of the negative. In fact, the depths of human negativity have not even begun to be plumbed. From the point of view of decision, the child begins to become an individual the first day he decides to say no. Until that moment, he is largely an appendage of his parents. From that moment on, he is on the road to becoming an individual with his own will, his own wishes.

While our own negativity may be a pain in the ass to us at times, when we think of its importance in our development we can see that we didn't become individuals until we first said no to an authority figure. Sometimes the only way we can bolster a shaky sense of self is by once more saying no to a parent, a husband or wife, a lover, even a child. At the point when I say no I am being my*self*, however small that self may feel at the moment.

"Hell is other people," Sartre wrote in *No Exit*. One of the most common sources of anger and unhappiness is that other people will not act the way we think they should. I remember the man who came to me and related the terrible tale of his wife's alcoholism and what it was doing to his life. The facts in themselves were dismaying enough, but this man's perception of them was guaranteed to make him miserable. "She controlled her drinking, all last week, then she got so smashed at the party she finally passed out. I just dread knowing that sooner or later she's going to get drunk."

I pointed out that the natural condition for an alcoholic is drunk—and here he was telling me that this one was making a superhuman effort to control her drinking some of the time. "Suppose," I suggested, "you were to start experiencing the times when she isn't drunk as times to be happy or at least tranquil? Instead of dreading her inevitable drunkenness, you could look upon it as the condition most alcoholics are in, far more often than your wife is at this point."

I don't mean to underestimate the pain people experience when they watch a loved one's progressive self-destruction from alcohol or other drugs. But trying to show how wrong the alcoholic is—or demonstrating that you are her victim—is almost certain to make her feel guilty, a great excuse to get drunk and make everyone even more miserable.

Many people, addicts more than most, are not free to make an independent choice unless we are ready to "join the resistance." We help ourselves—and them— much more when we understand rather than judge the reasons for their choice.

So much of our problem with other people comes from our not making the attempt to understand the other person's reality, what makes sense for them. We just try to get them to act the way we think they should act. This can tear *us* apart—and is remarkably ineffective in helping *them*. Probably this is why recovered alcoholics are so much more successful than psychotherapists (or husbands) when it comes to helping active alcoholics. Recovered alcoholics don't judge active alcoholics, they understand them. No body of explanations is asked for or needed, and they can get right down to the business of recovery.

No one, of course, judges us as severely as we judge ourselves. Try making a list of how many times during the course of one day you pass judgment on yourself—you'll be amazed at how long it is. On the other hand, if you try "joining the resistance" and thus getting rid of your hanging judge for a day, you're likely to be almost euphoric. Certainly you'll have a far better chance of changing the impossible problem into just another thing you have to deal with.

It may be more exciting to see every problem as open-heart surgery, but then every problem becomes a drama of major proportions. Yet the operative decision behind our dramatizations can be changed more easily than some. Such a change was set in motion with one profound insight on the part of a patient who frequently began her day with an academy award performance.

"I got up and felt awful," she told me. "I dropped the coffeepot on my toe, my boyfriend was going away, and I started crying. When he tried to comfort me I fell apart. I bemoaned all my bills, my unfinished work, my not being able to take a vacation. Five minutes later I was ready to declare bankruptcy and look for a smaller apartment. Finally I was so exhausted that I went back to bed.

"I woke up in a wonderful mood, remembered all that drama I'd gone through a few hours earlier—and it suddenly occurred to me that I'd gone through that whole scene just to tell myself to go back to bed because I was tired. What I did was dramatize: I'm tired and I want to go back to bed."

She was a very beautiful, beguiling woman, and she had dramatized the story so effectively that I thoroughly enjoyed it. "You're onto yourself now," I said. "You'll start learning to catch your act and cut it short some of the time. But if you get too good at it, you'll rob your friends of a lot of thrills!"

What happens to most of us, of course, is that after we start the performance we forget that it's a performance. It just takes over.

Once that happens, we really feel helpless—and we don't have to be. Instead, if our drama is making us unhappy—if we can't just go to bed and sleep it off—we can look for the operative decision behind the drama.

The best example I can think of is a drama that most of us know all too well: the Obsession. Now, whatever it is that's obsessing you—the man you're in love with, the woman you can't have, your diet—this particular drama is both painful to perform in and painful to witness. This one is guaranteed to stupefy all your friends. Pretty soon they will all have something very important to do when you want to talk about "it." You may even have to pay someone like me to listen to you when you want to talk about it.

Now if you can stop obsessing for even a moment about your obsession, you're likely to discover your operative decision. You're likely, in most cases, to find out that what consumes most of your waking thoughts is actually a mask for something you don't want to think about that's even worse. Only of course it isn't worse, it's just that you made a decision not to think about it and in order to blot it out of your mind you developed this obsession.

A colossal waste of time and energy—and a typical sentence passed by the hanging judge. If we didn't have that merciless bastard in our heads intoning "shoulds" and making everything seem like forced labor—it's no wonder we want to escape—then we might be able to attend to the task at hand and even enjoy it. Instead, we use measures as desperate as any criminal's, as dramatic as any actor's, to avoid his judgment.

I'm a little absentminded and sometimes forget or misplace things. My co-author took me to lunch, and as she went to pay the check I saw her frown and sigh. "I've lost my wallet, I must have left it at the drugstore." She looked stricken; I could almost see the judge raising the gavel above her head. "Forgive yourself," I said, and her expression immediately changed to a sheepish smile. "No use beating myself up, let's go look for it," she said. I'm so quick to spot the judge in that situation—because I have to kick his ass ten times a day or *I'd* get a life sentence for forgetfulness.

If you don't kick his ass, if you don't stand up to that voice of judgment, you really do commit crimes against humanity—your own and others. You make yourself and the people around you miserable, you diminish yourself, you kill off your spirit. Take it from someone who knows him: the judge would rather you be right than happy. "Forgive yourself." Maybe next time you'll see him coming.

In this chapter I have tried to identify some of the operative decisions that can sabotage our happiness or peace of mind. It's worth trying to find our own operative decisions if we suspect that our lives could be even a little more satisfying.

Whether we know it or not, many of us decided as children that we were too special to get along happily in this world. Maybe we were told that our potential was out of whack—we were over-achievers or we were underachievers. After that arraignment, our hanging judge started to wield the gavel. Ever since then we have deemed ourselves deficient or excessive in the cruel canon of our own minds. Rarely has anything been deemed sufficient.

Even worse than warped potential is perfectionism. Sufficiency, to a perfectionist, means failure. The perfectionists can go through life with a virulent case of the "shoulds," guaranteed to make themselves and anyone who cares about them tired. *Striving* for perfection, on the other hand, can be very useful—if we don't attack ourselves when we don't live up to an impossible demand.

Still others of us suffer from a consuming need to control things, including ourselves. Anything that eludes our control is a source of intolerable anxiety.

Then there's my Uncle Boris. In the labor unions in the 1920s there was a fierce struggle between the right and left wings. While the right was in power, Uncle Boris was an ardent leftist. Then the left wing took control of his particular union, and Boris became a rightist.

He joined a temple in order to fight against the administration there, even though Boris wasn't a religious man. As soon as he led a group from the congregation out of the place, he quarreled with his followers and left them. Uncle Boris's decision, of course, was to be different, to be in constant and total rebellion. I must say he had a very eventful life.

All of the operative decisions—under/over-achievement, perfectionism, rebellion, God of Control, doormat, whatever—are self-motivated. They originate with us. Just recognizing that fact can show us that we have the ability to decide and choose. Or redecide (like Boris). Or we can decide to soften a decision's effect on our lives. Or we can even change it.

Here's a chance to catch your own act, wake up and look at yourself, listen to yourself . . . and decide whether or not your decisions are contributing happiness to your life.

Step II: Find the Decision(s) Behind the Problem

- Think of someone you're always happy to be with.

- Think of someone who seems always happy to be with you.

- Remember a time in school when you were singled out for praise.

- Think of a time in school when you were criticized for something, and you stopped doing it.

- Think of a time when you ignored a piece of severe criticism, and lived to tell the tale.

- Think of a time you were ashamed of yourself, and figure out whether anybody noticed.

- Remember an occasion when you were pleased with yourself, and nobody knew.

- Try to remember the last time you laughed out loud, and why.

- Think of something you haven't done well enough, and plan to leave it the way it is.

- Think of something that doesn't have to be done well, and plan to improve it just for fun.

- Remember the very best piece of advice you ever got: if one person was responsible, write him or her a note.

- Listen to a few radio call-in talk shows, and ask yourself if your own problems are really exceptional.

- Figure out whether the people you try to impress with your behavior are impressed.

- See if you can figure out what impresses people about you when you're not trying.

- Ask yourself if what you spend the most nonworking hours doing each day is any fun.

- Think of what you'd most like to spend your nonworking hours doing, and decide to do it this afternoon.

5

Step III: Find the Context for the Original Decision (Ask Yourself When It Was Made)

JULIO was a small, compact Mexican artist who never tried to contain his feelings—he filled the classroom with alternating waves of happiness and pain. His English was adequate, but it was his face, a tragic mask, that most eloquently expressed his painful dilemma.

"I can no longer paint," he told us. "The colors paralyze me. I am dumb like a dog." I watched the reactions of people in the class. The women wanted to touch him, to soothe him, and the men shook their heads sadly.

Julio had come in desperation to my class in Direct Decision Therapy seeking help. "I come from a small village across the border," he said. "My family is very poor, eight brothers and sisters, we always live on a farm. All but me they are still there, so hopeless, but I leave and they think I am their hope. I think this too. Now, just when I can change everything for them, I am hopeless too." By now the room was all but shut down in mourning.

"So how did you get from there to here, Julio?" I asked. "Aside from not being able to paint, you look in pretty good shape to me."

A teacher in grade school, he told us, had noticed a drawing he made and praised him. "I will become an artist," he decided. "A great artist, the best ever."

I was not surprised by this piece of marvelous, grandiose self-esteem. Nearly every truly creative person has it. He gets an idea; he may know perfectly well that other people have had that idea, but he doesn't care. He knows that he is going to do it better than anybody ever did it before. That grandiosity is highly useful to him.

Julio's teacher kept up the encouragement, and Julio splashed the startling primary colors of Mexican folk art over canvas after canvas. From the beginning, he never got a lukewarm reaction to his work. Not only that, his goal was so clear, his enthusiasm so infectious that he really couldn't remember any obstacles he had overcome. In reality he had hitchhiked to San Diego, worked as a busboy in a restaurant, and attended art classes and painted in every minute of his spare time.

None of this seemed a hardship to Julio. Any circumstances that allowed him to paint were considered the highest good fortune. The combination of his talent and his ebullient, engaging personality opened doors in the art world. In fact, he was about to be given a major exhibition at the moment his painting paralysis hit him.

He was an interesting type to me, smart and pragmatic, filled with energy and the sure knowledge of what worked for him. He had experienced his life up to then, filled with material deprivation and backbreaking work, as one of good luck. He still didn't have any money—and so, knowing that he needed help in a hurry, he had offered himself as a guinea pig in return for free therapy.

Julio obviously was miserable being unhappy. Not everybody is, but unhappiness was not a state of mind he was familiar with or enjoyed. It was his discomfort over his own unhappiness that made me feel so optimistic about helping him.

"So all your life, things have gotten better and better for you. And you've gotten better and better. What else is there now but to be perfect?"

Julio looked at me with a glimmer of understanding. "And there is something else I haven't told. I cannot paint, yes, but I cannot fuck now either." The tragic mask descended again. "My girlfriend is very passionate because I am very good, you know. Even when I am tired, I make myself."

"Why, Julio? Why do you do it even when you're tired?"

"I am Mexican," he said, as if that explained everything. "I do it for '*La rasa.*'" The class laughed and Julio grinned, delighted to be understood.

"So everytime you fuck, you're doing it for the entire republic of Mexico," I said. "The reputation of the whole country depends on how well you paint and how well you fuck."

Julio nodded vigorously.

"I want to know when you decided you had to be perfect, Julio?"

He looked at me and thought for a minute. Then he said, "When I was praised for painting so long ago by my teacher. Because I thought—I *knew*—that this was the way out for me and my family. I knew always that I was good, but I knew also I had so much against me and so far to go that I had to be better than good to get there."

"You had to be perfect."

"Yes, perfect. And I always did get better, and I loved everything I did that let me leave the farm behind and paint. And now I finally have the big exhibition coming, it's my big chance to be judged by the best, to really be the great artist, and . . . I am afraid."

"You know, Julio, you could be judged to be the greatest painter in the world—greater than Rivera, greater than Picasso—and still not measure up to your idea of perfect. Because that's the problem with this thinking—the word 'measure.' You will always be able to set the limit a little out of your reach, as long as you're alive. Because the only thing after perfection is death. Once you get there, then there's no place to go."

Julio nodded, slowly this time.

"So I want you to do something for me. I want you to paint me a bad picture."

Gone was the tragic mask. Julio looked shocked and pained. "Please, that I cannot do."

"You came here for help and I'm telling you that your assignment for this class is to paint me a bad picture. If you look at it as a job you're doing, maybe you can do it. Then I'll tell you what to do next. For now, I'm telling you we can't proceed with the therapy until you paint me a bad picture."

Julio came to the class the next week and displayed his homework for us. You didn't have to know much about art to know the painting was terrific.

"I thought I asked you to paint me a bad picture."

He grabbed me and roared with laughter, thumping me on the back. "You knew I couldn't paint a bad picture!"

The painting turned out to be the most highly praised in Julio's exhibition. The whole class, myself included, felt as though they had helped liberate a great artist and joined his following.

Julio's problems cleared up with the realization that it was impossible for him to do anything he loved to do badly—painting, making love, even living.

Julio, who did things full out, all the stops pulled, had decided that he had to be perfect. Fortunately, he had also decided to do whatever it took for him to achieve his goals. His pragmatism had been so consistently rewarded that when I suggested he paint a bad picture the pragmatism set him into motion—even though the assignment went deeply against the grain of his perfectionism. It was clear to me that with Julio, pragmatism would always win out.

I love success stories, and I love remembering Julio's. I also remember it because it is a very clear example of two life decisions, pragmatism and perfectionism, which were compatible for a long time and then temporarily clashed. Once the pragmatist won the battle, Julio was able to experience and give even greater satisfaction to himself and those around him.

Human infants, upon entering this world, are among the weakest animals on earth. Few other animals are so defenseless, so completely unprepared for independent existence. We have to be taken care of by the people around us; we can't survive on our own. As we're growing up, a certain anxiety, a memory of this fundamental inadequacy, rarely leaves us. For a long period all our needs were taken care of. No matter how deprived we think we were as children, we really weren't, because if we had been truly deprived we wouldn't be alive.

Some of us define a relationship of love as one in which we will be treated, as grownups, the way we were as infants—our needs attended to without our having to ask. That unacknowledged expectation is deeply buried. It's also likely to take the form of a poignant, pointless life decision.

There's another decision we make—this one consciously—when we are very young. We decide that our parents can read our minds. We're not so far off base, either. The minds of children aren't hard to follow, especially your own children.

So when I work with couples, again and again I hear the refrain: If he/she really loved me, he/she would know what I want.

"Did you ask for it?"

"No, why should I?" Or even, "No, if I have to ask for it, that takes the pleasure out of getting it. It's like asking for a birthday present."

Male, female, it doesn't matter. Every so often we find that infant mask, then we pull it over our heads like a paper bag and wait to have our minds read, our needs attended to, our wishes fulfilled. All this is supposed to happen by our smiling—or, if in a different mood, crying. Or even by our wishing. When it doesn't happen, the infant in us is provoked to the point of rage.

The payoffs for this life decision, one of the most common ones, are very often negative. We become dependent and permit our feeling of well-being to derive from others. We give away our power.

Like so many life decisions, this one is both logical and unreasonable. It's just not reasonable to expect our adult love objects to be able to anticipate our needs and wishes the way our parents did. It's a lot easier to ask for what you want, of course. It either works, or you find out why not.

This is just one of the life decisions made in childhood that can make us card-carrying members of the Cargo Cult. The context for this decision is always the same: we decide that the people who love us should know what we want because our parents knew. But awareness of the decision and the context in which it was made can give us the opportunity to make another choice.

The same dynamic holds for operative decisions as well. They, too, are often made in childhood—and awareness of decision and context can enable us to change them. I made one of these decisions in the fourth grade. I wrote a composition my teacher liked very much, so much that she wanted to send it to the principal's office—on top of the stack, which is where the very best essay in the class always went. I was enormously excited at the prospect, and when she told me I would have to copy it over first, I set about the task. (In this school, as in so many, neatness counted more than content.)

For two days I sat at the back of the classroom, hunched over my sloppy work, trying desperately to make it neat. The process was sheer torture. When I finally gave it to the teacher she shook her head sadly and slipped it into the stack, third down from the top.

Here, obviously, is the context in which my operative decision not to rewrite was made. After this discovery, be assured that I was eager to challenge the fear. Alas, as with so many decisions I have made, the need to change that original decision faces me again and again—with every new book. (I didn't say Direct Decision Therapy would make life easy.)

The point is, decisions *can* change and still produce happiness—or misery, as the case may be. In the past, I have decided to rewrite if necessary (it always seemed to be necessary), and for this book I decided "no." If my co-author had materialized a book or two sooner, those decisions might have been different. You see, each decision was the right one at the time. This is important, because we don't need to feel that when we change an operative decision it's forever.

When we decide to change a *life* decision, the payoffs are usually so positive that we want it to be "forever." And, usually, we don't have to remake a new life decision; when it's changed, it stays changed.

This was the case with Neal, a patient who had a rather poetic look about him—handsome, sensitive features and a slim, graceful body. He was genuinely perplexed by his behavior.

"I was at an Outward Bound sort of weekend, and one of the women, a very fat woman named Daphne, was doing a godawful exercise where you hang suspended upside down from a rope strung across a ravine. You pull yourself across, and of course the heavier you are the lower the rope dips and the harder it is to make it to the other side because you're pulling yourself uphill.

"Anyway, I was watching Daphne struggle. Maybe twenty or thirty people were cheering her on, but I stopped watching—it was just too painful. She looked like a beached whale flipping from side to side. I knew she wasn't going to be able to make it, and I walked away to the other side of a hill. After a while the noise stopped and a small group of people came by me, talking and laughing. 'Hey, Neal, why are you looking so sad?'—it seems people have been asking me that all my life. Anyway, at the time I thought how insensitive people are and I said, 'Because of Daphne.

I'm upset that she couldn't make it.' The guy said, 'What do you mean? We were all right there, and she made it, she's terrific.' And then they walked on and forgot about me.

"Suddenly I realized I do that all the time. I look at a situation and decide it's going to be sad and most of the time don't even check to find out the truth. Do you think I just want to be sad?"

We didn't have to look long to find the context for Neal's life decision to be sad. As a beautiful, sensitive little boy, he had been lavished with attention and sympathy every time he experienced sadness—whether the occasion was a dropped ice cream cone or his bicycle's being stolen. As an adult, he still sometimes got the payoffs of love and attention for his sorrow, but he increasingly began to find life lived on such a muted level unsatisfactory. He was able to use his awareness to change that life decision, permanently. It took some practice before he could catch himself in advance of the "sad" situation—at first, his awareness of the life decision and its context only enabled him to see that he'd "done it again." Eventually, however, Neal became a happy man, thoughtful and sensitive but not inappropriately sad.

Life decisions can be confusing to all of us. In trying to sort them out, we need to look at our present behavior and ask ourselves whether we're reacting automatically—in a way that is damaging to ourselves and others—or having a spontaneous reaction to an experience. One way out of the confusion is to look and see if a circumstance and your reaction to it occur often in your life. If you can see a pattern, then you have an opportunity to look deeper. None of us has to live a life run by old and currently inappropriate decisions if we don't want to.

Peter was a dynamic, dramatic trial lawyer who was one of the fastest talkers I ever met. He was much in demand professionally, perhaps because he could first anesthetize and then hypnotize the jury with his barrage of words and gestures.

Almost every time he came to see me, Peter would have a tale of crisis to tell. And it was always a terrible crisis. There was a chance of his being brought up on charges before the Ethics Committee by the State Bar Association, or the Internal Revenue was after him, or the Traffic Court (Peter ran red lights). Every time one problem cleared up, a new one reared its head. "This has got to stop," he would say.

The reason he'd gone for help in the first place was that his family was sick of life in the crisis zone. His teenagers turned up their radios when he came into the room, and his wife had stopped paying any attention whatsoever to his dramatizations. So Peter came to me for an audience.

When he temporarily ran out of disasters, he would spend the time impressing me with his high I.Q. and his professional reputation. I suggested that since he was indeed smart and successful he might be less disaster-prone if he stopped trying to impress people, which possibly irritated them into making life difficult for him. "Don't make yourself so big, you're not so small," I said, passing on Reik's advice to one of his patients.

"I know, I know, but you have to remember that I couldn't take tests when I was a kid and so at first they thought I was retarded."

"Look at what a great opportunity you passed up. You could have been a dishwasher or a mechanic, then you wouldn't have had all these problems. Dishwashers are hardly ever brought up before ethics committees."

"But you don't understand. One doctor recommended that I be put in a mental hospital!"

"So what's wrong with mental hospitals? Look how nice life would be for you, you wouldn't have to worry about anything. I know mental patients who have regular relapses just so they don't have to go out and face the world. If you're so smart, you'd be in a mental hospital."

He said no, he could never do that, they'd order him around.

Since my tactics weren't working—Peter had yet to crack a smile—
I asked him what had happened after he was pronounced nuts.

"My mother took me to another doctor, and the next thing I
knew she threw a flower vase at him. I think the doctor had implied
that she was responsible for my craziness."

I suggested that maybe his mother hadn't liked what the doctor
said about her little boy. Maybe she had believed him to be as
smart and talented as he turned out to be. "All the forces of the
universe may not be lined up against you after all, Peter."

Peter wasn't crazy about that interpretation. It's tough, coming
to grips with the fact that your parents loved you and wanted to
protect you. Especially if you are blaming all of your difficulties on
them.

"You know, Peter, I think you may be a sufferer." I threw that
out to see how he would react. "You may have found that the best
way you could get along in your family was to have a crisis."

He was thoughtful—even quiet—for a few moments. Then he
said, "It's true my mother was a wild woman. She had an uncon-
trollable temper if I did anything to make her mad, but if I was
hurting or in trouble, she'd come to the rescue."

Now, Peter's decision to suffer had been made long ago and was
deeply ingrained. The behavior resulting from such a decision is
rarely examined, and hard to give up. When Peter's wife stopped
responding to his crises, he was deeply hurt. Having dutifully
soothed and supported him for years, she no longer would even
listen to him.

I knew why she wouldn't listen. Peter was a Protestant and his
wife was Jewish. She'd had five thousand years of experience with
real suffering behind her. She lost patience and tuned him out—a
shocking withdrawal of a payoff, which had sent him to me.

"I do feel better," he said gratefully. Then his brow furrowed and
he said, "I just wonder how I'm ever going to get over this."

"See? There you go, suffering again." He laughed, and I began to be very encouraged about his prospects for happiness. "You know Jews really know how to suffer," I said. "We can produce tragedies. Your suffering is more in the mosquito league. A mere nuisance. Know your audience, Peter—go apologize to your wife and tell her you're not going to do your suffering number unless you can come up with a tragedy."

Peter's decision to suffer, once we looked at the context, was a survival mechanism. It was the only way he could see to control his mother's temper, to keep it aimed at an enemy outside. Better she threw things at the doctor than at him.

We all have an ingrained need to rebel against our parents. Our survival doesn't depend on it—but our maturity does. Many of us are still walking around with our rebelliousness trapped inside us. We haven't been allowed—or, like Peter, we didn't dare—to act it out. This unresolved childhood rebelliousness then sneaks out in very damaging ways, making it impossible for the grownup rebel to take orders gracefully or even at all from a foreman, a manager, an editor. It's interesting that Peter continually provoked authorities to come after him—the Ethics Committee, the IRS, the traffic authorities.

After we spent some time discussing all of this, Peter's act lost a lot of its steam. He just couldn't throw himself into it the way he used to. We could then look at his role in creating very real disasters—though it pained him and made him "suffer" a bit, he began to change his behavior toward these authoritarian bodies and stopped playing the victim.

I've said that once you take a look at the context in which it was made, no life decision or operative decision seems truly bizarre. I must say that Shirley, a patient sent to me in response to my request for someone willing to be hypnotized, put this theory of mine to a severe test.

I was teaching in New York at the time, at an institute connected with an outpatient treatment service. The treatment center staff was a little reluctant to produce a subject—until they hit upon the idea of sending me Shirley. Here, they felt sure, was somebody who couldn't be damaged by hypnotism. In fact (they didn't tell me this) they had already planned to hospitalize her—having determined, through a battery of tests and weeks of observation, that she was not a good prospect for outpatient treatment.

Shirley came into the room in a frenzy of activity. Her hands seemed to have a life of their own, traveling like two moths to her hair, her face, her waist, then back to the hair—up, down, around, up. She made me dizzy, especially when she came and stood right in front of me.

"Do you want me?" she demanded. "Nobody wants me."

In a high-pitched, squeaky voice she told us that she had been rejected by somebody important to her. I figured he probably was just exhausted from watching Shirley in perpetual motion. Looking at her now, I wanted to capture those hands before I gave in to motion sickness. Instead, I just said, "What do you want, Shirley?"

"If only I could sleep. That's what I want, to sleep."

"Why can't you sleep?"

"I'm afraid a dead person will enter my body while I'm asleep. I know a girl that happened to and she got terrible headaches."

Now that didn't seem to me like the worst consequence of having a dead person in your body, but I asked Shirley more about it and she described leaving her body and observing it—astral projection, she called it.

It seemed to me that we were progressing at a terrific rate. I've treated insomniacs for months on end before they ever get around to mentioning the "voices" that are keeping them awake. Then we treat the voices. Shirley had spun us from rejection to insomnia to astral projection in the first ten minutes.

She went on to describe her life on the fringe, the drug use, the far-out sex—not on an astral level but distinctly kinky. And she never once sat still.

"Shirley," I said, "I can hypnotize you into an LSD trip. Would you like that?"

"Oh, yes," she said, and the hands even came in for a landing in her lap. Having hypnotized people into druglike states before, I wasn't surprised when I had Shirley in an LSD-type trance within five minutes.

"What do you see?" I asked her.

Everything about her had settled into repose. Her face was relaxed into a perfectly ordinary blank stare, just like someone sitting on a subway seat.

"Nothing," she said.

"Nothing at all?"

"No. Nothing."

"All right, you mentioned you want to be an actress. So think of yourself onstage in front of an audience."

"Okay, I can do that."

She started to smile. I asked her, "What's going on now?"

"I'm smiling," she said. "And bowing."

"What's the audience doing?"

"Applauding."

"Terrific. Now see if you can see some kind of a scene, see if you can create a play starring yourself that expresses something you want the world to know about you."

No matter how hard I tried, using a variety of techniques including those that work with even the least imaginative patient, Shirley couldn't see anything except herself smiling and bowing. After ten minutes or so I took her out of the trance.

"You know," I said, "you're the most unusual case I ever saw in my life. Most people act sane on the outside and have at least a certain amount of craziness on the inside. You're as crazy as they come—on the outside. But inside, you're completely sane."

Shirley looked at me. No gestures, no histrionics—she started to cry softly. "So you know, huh?"

"I think so, Shirley. But why don't you tell us about it."

"I've always known I was ordinary, so completely boring and ordinary. When I was fourteen, I decided I was going to be different. I started hanging around all the freaks in school—they scared me, but it was worth it if I could learn to be different and interesting. I didn't really mean to be taken for crazy at first, but if that was what I could do to be different and interesting then I thought it was better than just being plain boring me."

She seemed so dejected at being unmasked that I tried to make her feel better. "Look how different you really are, Shirley. You went from being diagnosed as a paranoid schizophrenic ready for hospitalization to being a perfectly sane woman in one session. You're very articulate about your history and your decision. You're not even nervous any more—you're sitting there composed, even though you're sad. I think you'll do fine without the crazy act."

She left the session to try out her less taxing shtick—the magically cured patient. By the third time I saw her she was obviously in charge of herself, speaking quite calmly, answering questions from the class clearly and thoughtfully. The class members went after her in a variety of ways—and the more they went after her, the more disturbed some of them sounded and the saner the patient sounded.

They asked her what would happen if she got rejected again, and her answer was wonderful.

"Well, I'd feel sorry about it, and I'd probably cry for a while. I don't like to be rejected—does anybody? But there's no sense in carrying on the way I did before. I was going on a whole psychotic trip and it's not necessary."

She seemed relieved to be rid of her crazy persona. The interesting thing is, she had never forgotten that it was a performance, the way most people do (like Irwin the jeweler). She was eaten up with fear of being found out and so uncomfortable with her act that she developed all those weird body mannerisms, which really kept people at a distance, isolating her far more than her true, "ordinary" personality possibly could have.

I'm not trying to suggest that all people with serious problems deliberately decide to put on a performance. Often, as was the case with Irwin, the act takes over and the star forgets it's just a drama he has created. There have been far greater performances in my office than I have ever seen in the theater. Some of them by myself.

A few years after I started practice, I was influenced by two books: Lucy Freeman's *Fight Against Fears* and Robert Lindner's *The Fifty-Minute Hour.* Lucy Freeman's book is a description of her own analysis. It's a touching, sensitive story in which the analyst is depicted as kindly and friendly. I warmed to that role model. *The Fifty-Minute Hour* is a thrill a minute with the analyst, Robert Lindner, stalking through the patient's psyche picking up clues for the breathtaking denouement. I warmed to the idea of myself as supersleuth.

In the beginning I couldn't decide just how I wanted to play my analyst role, so I switched back and forth. When I played the kindly, friendly analyst, I got very nice feedback and patients let me know how warm, kind, and friendly I was. When I played supersleuth, they were impressed by my startling discoveries.

There was only one problem. They didn't necessarily get any better with either method. I try always to remember now: There can only be room for one actor in the room with the couch.

What role are you playing in your life? What scenes bring out the shameless ham in you? We find them so easy to spot in others, so difficult to get a handle on in ourselves. Tracing back our behavior to an original decision and the context in which it was made is a little like solving a mystery. It's interesting, and finding them can help us get on with our lives free of some leftover pattern of happiness-blocking behavior. But we don't *have* to find them in order to get on with our lives and change a leftover pattern. It's interesting, it's not essential.

Life decisions and operative decisions, we have seen, are usually well disguised. Julio's perfectionism, Neal's sadness, and Peter's suffering were all coping behaviors that provided payoffs. Because their roles were no normal to all four of these people, they lost perspective on themselves and the way they affected the people in their lives.

It's helpful to be able to zero in on a precise occurrence in your past and see the context in which you made a decision that no longer makes sense. But as I said, it's not essential. And context doesn't have to be specific—approximate will do just fine.

What you may want to do here, with the following list, is to think of any behavior patterns that may be keeping you from being happy. Then think back—to adolescence, to childhood, to whatever part of your life seems most likely to have a bearing on the pattern you're concerned about. Somewhere in there is the context of your life decisions and your operative decisions.

You'll be happier for having thought through whatever you can recall that made you *un*happy. And at the very least, thinking about your life history and behavior patterns will increase your self-awareness. That, all by itself, will expand your ability to choose the happy alternative.

Step III: Find the Context for the Original Decision (Ask Yourself When It Was Made)

- Try to recall your earliest memory.

- Think of a time when you made your parents unhappy.

- Think of a time your parents made you happy.

- Remember playing dress-up and what sort of clothes you most enjoyed putting on.

- Remember schoolyard fights and arguments. Whose side were you on? The bullies? The underdogs?

- Remember a teacher who influenced the course of your life.

- Remember a time when you were very young and a grownup said you were good at something.

- Remember being misunderstood as a child. Ask yourself if you could have misunderstood the situation.

- Think of some ways in which you are like your father.

- Think of some ways in which you resemble your mother.

- Think about what came easily to you as a child and what was really hard.

- Try to recall your happiest first memory.

- Remember the first time you were unhappy. Think what you would do about that situation now.

- Think about what you did to be happy as a child.

- Remember what you did to get over being unhappy as a child.

- Recall the time(s) as a child when you ran away from home, or wanted to. Remember why.

- Remember why you came back.

6

Step IV: List the Payoffs for the Decision

CANDICE was a young woman who came to see me because she was afraid she would commit suicide. She kept finding herself stuck in a bog of self-loathing where she had to listen to the voice inside her suggest that she just end it all. (I don't call him the hanging judge for nothing.)

Here she was, a long-limbed, lovely blonde with soft blue eyes, a soft clear voice, and a laugh (when we could find it) that sounded like wind chimes. And the judge wanted to hang her.

Candice had started out in the sixties as a flower child, East Coast version. Her mother was a crusading civil-rights worker, a tireless political activist more involved in causes than in home life. Candice's father, an accountant, was a respectable but dispirited man who had turned more and more to alcohol to provide the satisfaction in his life. He loved Candice in his sad, boozy way, and in one of his more sober moments he suggested that she seek professional help.

Candice had been on the fringes of the drug culture while at college in New York, though she did not take drugs herself until she fell in love with the man she eventually married. Jerry was a flamboyant counterculture star who doubled as the local pusher. He was arrogant, handsome, and manipulative, able to dance circles around the dangers of his illegal trade. His exploits thrilled Candice and she became addicted to him and to the excitement he brought to her life. The fact that this king of the local pushers had chosen her as his consort made her willing to do anything for him. He married her and they left for Europe, ready to conquer the Old World with their hip and savvy ways and their all-American good looks.

Predictably, the world was tougher out there where they didn't speak the language, and the sun never seemed to shine. It seemed easier to confront the strangeness through a haze of hash. But then Jerry started solving his main problems through the main line. Jerry the pusher became Jerry the junkie, and Candice became a call girl. She kept doing one more "favor" for Jerry—"until I get this new stash, then everything will be all right." She sort of knew it wouldn't be all right, but she loved him and, besides, there were no other jobs available over there without a work permit. Before long Jerry had stopped trying to get back on his feet, he was so well taken care of by Candice's new position off her feet. Jerry the junkie became Jerry the pimp.

Candice finally had to leave him, because when he needed a fix badly he would get violent and beat her up. Then neither one of them could work. And all this time Candice had her hanging judge beating her up inside as well. It was all too much.

She came back to New York, where one thing led to another and she found herself operating rather successfully as a call girl. That was when the judge started death-sentencing, and Candice's father started suggesting professional help.

"I feel so trapped," she said softly.

"Tell me something, Candice. Why did you go back to being a call girl when you came home to the States? Jerry was out of your life, you're smart and well educated, you could have gotten a legitimate job."

"Oh, I don't know, really. But I never learned to do anything I thought people would pay me to do. I have a good voice and I love to sing, but I've never been trained as a singer. I was an honor student at college, but what can you do with a B.A.? I guess I just went back to the life because it seemed so easy. You know I hate myself—don't you know I don't need you or anybody to tell me I'm worthless?"

"I don't think you're worthless, I just think you're stubborn. Now are you sure there are no payoffs for being a call girl here?"

Candice considered for a moment. "I thought I'd die when my mother found out," she said. "Was that awful! Now my dad's the only one in my family who'll speak to me. You know, my mother went bananas when she found out—she didn't say 'That's nice, dear,' and go off to one of her meetings this time. Why is she so down on me? She's supposed to be such a liberal!"

"Did you ever think maybe there was no point in being a call girl unless your mother found out? At least she paid attention to what you were doing. I wrote my doctoral dissertation on call girls, and some of them used to send newspaper clippings home to their moms when they got busted."

Candice laughed, and while I listened to the wind chimes I watched the expression on her face. She had the satisfied look you see on the face of a five-year-old who's just gotten away with something. Then she sobered.

"Look at my mom, spending all her time uplifting the world. What about me? Now she won't even speak to me. I'm hopeless."

We went on for many sessions like this. Candice was a dedicated victim, but little by little—in between the "I-hate-myself" and the "I-can't-help-it" routines—she began to see her decision and why she had made it. It's very hard to give up being a victim, even if you realize you decided to be one. The payoff for your decision is that you don't have to take responsibility for your life.

The more Candice was able to see that she had decided to be a victim, long ago, the more uncomfortable she became. It was a tough predicament. If she decided to change, she would have to forgive her mother for being the person she was (and wasn't). For a long time, proving her mother wrong had been very important to Candice.

It became less important as she became better able to experience her anger toward her mother. Here she'd gone to all this trouble, making a drastic operative decision to drop out and become so self-destructive that her mother would *have* to pay attention and take care of her—and Mom wasn't even speaking to her, much less spending all her time worrying about her daughter. All of this had brought Candice to the point of considering the ultimate attention getter: suicide. What a payoff, pushing up daisies for Mom. ("I just know she wouldn't even look after my grave.")

It took a long time before Candice could express her anger at the way her drama had flopped; even longer before she could consider making some decisions that would put her in control of her future. She started laughing a little at the lengths to which she had gone—and at the strength her mother had shown in resisting her daughter's manipulations.

"Your mother doesn't strike me as the only strong one in the family," I said. "Look how strong and stubborn *you* are. Look how many years you have been going public so Mom will give up public life. This is a fantastic show of strength, when you think about it. If you keep it up you just might win—you might hold out long enough to break her down and destroy both of you."

Candice laughed heartily. Then she said, quite seriously, "I guess I am strong. But where do I go from here? I may be smart but I don't have any skills—I couldn't even be a secretary. All I know how to do is sell myself."

"So what? Lawyers sell themselves . . ."

As I've described it in chapter 2, this is the moment in which Candice seized upon the word "lawyer" and announced she was going to become one. It's what I call a "teachable" moment. She had suddenly let in the truth about who was responsible for her life, and that truth created a moment in which she could make a decision that would drastically change it.

I knew that Candice had reached this point, but I didn't know her mind would shut like a steel trap on the first attractive alternative she heard. As best I could see, the law appealed to her because it *seemed* terribly respectable. It was also terribly challenging. I enjoyed my own surprise at the swiftness of her decision—and gladly abandoned my skepticism when she took all that dogged determination she'd been using on her mother and used it to get into law school.

This time, Candice was fully aware that the decision was hers. She did all the research and took pains to educate me about each step she was going through in order to reach her goal. She got early experience in litigation arguing with me, and passed her bar exams with flying colors.

Along with Candice's new view of herself and new profession came many other changes. She joined a Baptist church choir and built a reputation for herself as an ensemble singer on the church-concert circuit. Since her mother was a confirmed atheist, Candice's new avocation was almost as hard for her to take as her daughter's former success at the oldest profession.

Early on in her law career, Candice was afraid that a former "client" would recognize her and expose her.

"Don't worry," I couldn't resist counseling. "They'll never know you with your clothes on."

She groaned. "A lot you know about it. Call girls aren't just hired for their bodies, you know. More johns than I'd care to remember know me with my clothes on."

"Look, I was joking—and anyway, the clothes aren't the same. You not only have a different life now, you look completely different. Your hair style is different, your make-up, the way you dress, your whole manner. From spacy call girl to dynamic professional woman—what a metamorphosis! Practically everything about you has changed. Except your mother."

As it turned out, it wasn't my reassurance but a wonderful coincidence that convinced Candice she didn't have to worry.

"I rushed into court late," she told me one afternoon. "I hardly had time to look over my brief, and while I'm whispering with my client the judge came out of chambers, and—there he was! In his robes, one of my johns from years back!" She could hardly finish the story for laughing. "Can you believe it? And all this time I was afraid someone would finger *me*! He must have died when he looked down from his bench and saw me. But I want you to know, we went through the whole thing straight-faced."

"Did it ever occur to you maybe he really didn't recognize you?"

"Look, he had a costume on and I recognized him. Do you think it's possible he didn't know? Well, anyway, I won the case, Harold, and I'll never know for sure which talent swayed him."

This incident was the most enjoyable for me of many in Candice's success story. Somehow, more than anything it seems to represent a nose thumbed at the hanging judge.

It's interesting that we can trace so many of our decisions back to childhood. And somebody's always getting things switched around "up there" or down here in the hospital nursery, because so many of us end up with the wrong parents. Candice was looking for a Jewish mother and got stuck with a political activist busy tending to the world. I can't tell you how many of my patients would have been thrilled to have Candice's mother instead of their own. "If she'd only let me alone for just five minutes . . ." "If she'd just get involved in something else . . ."

Unfortunately, as was the case with Candice, the decisions made in response to your parents can narrow a life's purpose down to proving them wrong, or proving yourself right, or showing them you can make it, or justifying yourself. . . . It's absolutely amazing how much energy we can put into these unconscious goals—energy that could otherwise go into increasing our happiness and satisfaction.

I had a patient who spent maybe 50 percent of his time and energy covering up for the fact that he could never—and I mean never—get anywhere on time or finish anything within an imposed time frame. Jake simply had to do it his way, which got him into endless explanations and, from time to time, a lot of trouble. Whenever he had recycled his excuses so many times no one believed them any more, he had to change wives or friends or credit cards.

Since Jake wouldn't allow himself ever to be on time, he was always running. Finally he ran to me, exhausted and bewildered. By now he knew what he was doing (no one by now would let him forget it), but he didn't know *why* he was doing it, and he couldn't stop. Of course he couldn't make it to therapy on time either.

"Look," I said, "come when you feel you can. I'm sure you'll get just as much out of therapy by coming only for the last half hour."

Jake came on time after that. Now if I had said the same thing sarcastically instead of sincerely, he would have made a point of coming even later or maybe stopped coming altogether. I really did mean it sincerely, too—I stopped thinking I know what's best for patients a long time ago. Plus, I don't think manipulation works in the long run. If I don't have respect for the patient and some belief in his capacity to deal with his own problems, then there is no way I can offer any real help or guidance.

Jake obviously had decided to do something about his life decision—to be late and do things his way—or he wouldn't have come to see me in the first place. That's why I let patients make the decisions. Because if they have chosen the treatment, they've also chosen the consequences (the new payoffs) of feeling better and being able (deciding) to handle their own problems.

When Jake saw how much he was cheating himself by his

procrastination and constant juggling of responsibilities, he stopped the frantic activity long enough to find its source. His father had been a severe disciplinarian who insisted that Jake be meticulous about details, "a man of his word" as a boy of six. That meant, among other things, *be on time*. Jake, a very bright, very intense child, had often been so involved in activities that he was late for chores. His father had punished him, and Jake had felt wronged and rebellious. He decided to prove to his father that he would succeed in life whether he was on time or not.

He did end up making a lot more money than his father, who had been a construction foreman. But the more Jake procrastinated, the harder he had to work to achieve his ambition—which was, oddly enough, brain surgery. Now, nobody wants to rush a brain surgeon or get him rattled by calling him on tardiness. So after scrambling through medical school (late, of course), Jake settled down in his career—only to get in increasing amounts of trouble in other areas of his life, where people (like his third wife and the IRS) were not so understanding as his patients. "After all," Jake told me, "in the O.R. they can't start without me."

"So you've proved to your father that you can do it your way and succeed. Does he know?"

"He's dead."

"So what's the payoff now?"

"Well . . . after you've been a surgeon for a while and all these people treat you like God, it does begin to seem that the world revolves around you. A lot of doctors really get off on keeping people waiting, and maybe I'm one of them. . . . Seems sort of cheap thrills when I describe it that way."

"Never mind cheap, a payoff is a payoff. Can you see any payoffs in being on time?"

"Sure. The IRS might get off my back. My wife wouldn't divorce me, I could keep her. My two ex-wives and the children wouldn't be furious with me all the time—I could enjoy my kids. Yes, I can see a few payoffs."

Now Jake's payoffs had continued even when his behavior became a real problem. The rewards accruing to God-the-tardy-brain-surgeon were satisfying enough to keep him going even though he was beginning to experience a lot of losses—another wife, any fun with his kids, several friends, and his credit standing. (Jake made plenty of money. It just never was where it should be, and his financial records were a shambles.) Finally the combined threat of a tax evasion sentence and a third divorce brought his childhood decision and his adult reality into such a painful clash that he went for help.

As a patient, Jake was perceptive and quick to face facts—when he let himself stop running. He grew increasingly aware of how exhausting his rat race had become, especially after his father died.

"It's no wonder," I said. "You have to work much harder to get 'I'll show you, Dad' across through another medium besides telephone to Queens."

"I know. And what's the point?"

"You tell me."

"Now that I know what I'm up to, it certainly doesn't seem worth all the trouble it causes me. The price is just too high."

Usually, when payoffs for compulsive behavior become less rewarding (which often happens as we get older), the behavior disappears. Or, as in Jake's case, it eventually runs out of gas. The trouble is, if the energy fueling the behavior is running out and we get even one little payoff out of the blue, the unwanted behavior pattern can get revved up all over again.

When I was about four years old, I was taken to my aunt's graduation from high school on the Lower East Side. This was my first public appearance in a world I knew to be populated by universally admiring grownups. I got bored with sitting in my seat; I wanted to run around and show off, grab a little attention. The principal of this small Jewish school had seen my type before. He pointed his finger at me and said, "Keep quiet, you!"

In extremely clear tones, I called back to him: "You'd better not point your finger at me like that or I'll bite it off!" I was removed from the hall, kicking and screaming. But not before I noticed that both my parents were laughing. For several years after that I had the pleasure of hearing the story passed along: "He's so fresh, that Harold. Do you know what he did when he was just four . . ."

I already knew they thought I was a genius ("little genius" was how they referred to me), but to be a *fresh* little genius was practically a full-time job for a growing child. I managed, though, and the payoffs were good and bad. As you grow older, impertinence is not necessarily cute any more, and there were many times when I was fresh and *no one* was amused. But just when I would decide to go for a different sort of payoff (say, dignity), someone would reward an outrageous remark with a laugh, and the fresh kid would be back in residence. I am now seventy-three years old, and my fresh mouth still gets me in trouble occasionally—and, occasionally, gets me such a satisfying payoff that I may never abandon it entirely.

Which brings me to Gloria, an amateur sculptor who came to me in a deep depression. There were tears in her eyes and in her voice, all the time. She could hardly tell me what was wrong.

"He's such a wonderful man, and I love him so much. He's my husband, and to me he's the sexiest man alive, and . . . he just doesn't want me any more."

I took a good look at Gloria. Very exciting, very appealing, very inviting.

"You're obviously desirable," I said. "Did you ever think this might be his problem, not yours?"

"No, you don't understand. I want him and I just can't have him.

He still acts loving toward me in other ways, and I even think he still loves me. He just gets his sex somewhere else. I don't know what to do any more. It would be all right with him if I got *my* sex somewhere else, but I don't want other men. I want him. And I feel as though no one would find me desirable if he doesn't."

"If I may say so, Gloria, I find it hard to imagine the man who wouldn't find you desirable. Your problem might be that *you* don't find you desirable. Is that possible?"

"Yes . . . well, no. *He* doesn't. And my problem is that I'm depressed all the time. I've only done three pieces of sculpture in the last five months. It *hurts* that he doesn't want me."

"As I've said, that's his problem. Now we want to know what's your problem."

She was beginning to get exasperated by my obtuseness. She had stopped sniffling, though. As for me, I fell back on an old psychotherapeutic standby.

"I'd like you to describe to me what you're feeling right now."

"I'm depressed, and . . ."

"Forget the depression. Tell me what you're feeling, right now."

"I feel the way I did when I was little and nobody would play with me. I used to sit on the front steps and stare off into space. My mother accused me of sulking."

"What did she do besides that?"

"Well . . . she'd give me something to do, or sometimes she'd play with me herself. She could be a lot of fun."

"Are you sulking now?"

"*No!* I don't want to give up sex—I'm too young. And I don't want to get a divorce, I love my husband. . . . *Am* I sulking?"

"I don't know, but we may be getting somewhere. Do you want your husband to know that you don't have anyone to play with?"

Gloria looked a little sulky and sighed. "Of course he knows. I tell him."

"So maybe the payoff for this, ah, depression is that he knows you don't have anyone to play with. Now, do you think you decided to sulk—I mean, get depressed—to prove something to your husband?"

Gloria frowned, then let out a sigh of pure exasperation. "I didn't decide anything, Dr. Greenwald. I'm depressed because he makes me depressed, because he doesn't want me any more . . ." Her voice trailed off and the tears started to come on.

"Now I understand. You've been brainwashed. You know, you're the first patient I ever had with that problem, although I have read about it. Did you ever read *The Manchurian Candidate*? It's really a fascinating book."

"What *are* you talking about?"

"Well, you said you're depressed all the time, right?"

"Yes."

"And you said your husband makes you depressed. And that you never decided anything. You're just a victim of your husband's behavior, right?"

"Well . . ."

"Isn't that brainwashing? When a person's behavior is controlled by someone else, against that person's will? Unless of course you enjoy being depressed. Do you?"

"Of course I don't. Dammit, I'm miserable!"

"But, Gloria, your husband isn't here to appreciate how miserable he's making you. So there's no payoff. And you said you didn't decide to be depressed, to sulk, so you must have been brainwashed."

"*I have not been brainwashed!* I don't believe I'm having this conversation."

"Okay, I'll take your word for it. But since you didn't decide to be depressed, then maybe you don't have to be. Let's see. I'll tell you a few jokes . . ."

Silence. Then: "Are you sure you're Dr. Greenwald? Not some screwball who's tied him up and thrown him in the closet?"

Silence.

"You think I decided to sulk, don't you?"

"You know, you're lucky I just didn't leave and report you to the Better Business Bureau or something. You really take a lot of chances acting like that."

"You win some, you lose some. But look at the payoffs I get . . ."

Then Gloria and I got down to decisions.

Much of life is learning to deal with problems arising from our close relationships. Gloria had a real one in her husband's sexual neglect. But her response, depression (or sulking), wasn't helping the problem. If anything it was the response most likely to perpetuate his neglectful behavior. In fact, the more Gloria acted in accordance with a childhood decision to get her mother's attention when she didn't have a playmate, the more noticeably he failed to respond the way Gloria thought he should—and the more depressed she got.

The bad news is that we don't have any control over other people's behavior, especially our love objects' behavior. Unlike our parents, they always seem to learn ways to resist our manipulations.

A famous encounter technique, some years ago, was to have a person fall backward and be caught by a member of the group. The point was to learn to trust. That's valuable in its way, but I think the training would have been more valuable if the person fell backward and conked his head. It's more the way life is.

I couldn't treat Gloria for her husband's loss of desire (a very common complaint, by the way). But I could bring her anger to the surface and her humor out from hiding. As soon as she saw that she could make some decisions about her own responses—that there were alternatives, with more satisfying payoffs, to sulking or waiting around for her husband to change—she learned something even more valuable about herself. Gloria was using her depression about her husband's sexual coldness to mask a different problem —insecurity about her talent as a sculptor.

Now the lack of sex in her marriage was a real problem. But once we started dealing with the big problem of Gloria's creativity and how she really wanted to express herself, she barely summoned up enough interest to answer questions about her sex life. "Oh, that. Well, I can't do anything about it, now can I? But if this gallery is willing to take two more pieces . . ."

The fact is, problems come and go and come back again, and the surest way to the most satisfying payoffs is realizing that we've chosen the ones we have at the moment. Again, with the awareness comes the opportunity to choose a happier alternative.

If you are willing to take a look at your own payoffs, be careful about the tone. Your hanging judge is probably standing in his robes, ready to snarl, "All right, stupid, so you're depressed—what are the payoffs?" Kick him out of chambers. It's important to look at what you are doing without blaming or judging.

Remember, this behavior has worked for you so far, in some way, even though it may have made you suffer. If you can allow yourself the validity of your behavior (no matter how painful or damaging), you can allow yourself to see the truth about your payoffs instead of stirring up a lot of guilt. Guilt will only ensure that you keep on doing what you're doing.

Look at it this way: no matter how unhappy life has been for you so far, you have survived. You have coped. And you can, if you choose, sweeten things for yourself. Less salt, fewer wounds.

We cannot forget that most of our life decisions are made while we are still immature and dependent. We act on them later—much later, sometimes—when we have forgotten what they are, if we ever knew at all.

Now all life decisions and operative decisions have payoffs. Most of them are serviceable, and some work like well-oiled machinery. If they did not have any payoffs, they would disappear. The important question is: what is the best way to obtain the payoffs? Or, are you paying too high a price for too little? Many people find that the price they pay is more than the price they pay for therapy.

Once they show up in my office or classroom, no matter how nice-looking or well-dressed or well-spoken they are, I never ask them, "So how did a nice person like you get mixed up with a rumpled old shrink like me?" I find out what the behavior is that brought them in to see me. And then, as soon as I know a little about the behavior and the problems it creates, I ask the patient in one way or another, "What's the payoff?"

You can ask yourself the same question. Just asking it, in fact, provides a payoff.

Step IV: List the Payoffs for the Decision

See if any of these ring your payoff bell.

- If you tell people your troubles, they'll sympathize.

- If you tell people your troubles, they'll find something else to do.

- If people knew what you're really like, they wouldn't like you.

- When you let down your guard, people take advantage of you.

- When you let people see the real you, they like what they see.

- People like you because you're kind and helpful.

- Being kind and helpful makes you a doormat.

- Being kind and helpful makes you feel good.

- If you didn't do it on purpose, you didn't do it.

- If you don't do much, nobody will expect much of you.

- If you're hurting, nobody will care.

- If you're hurting, your friends will be supportive.

- Keeping up a front is the best way to survive.

- If you're sick, you won't have to take care of yourself.

- If you say no to a friend, you'll probably lose the friend.

- If you can't do it just right, it's better not to do it at all.

- If you don't try to do it right, you'll never know if you're any good at it at all.

- You'd like some help, but none is ever offered.

- Ask for help, and you might get it.

- When you get help, you give someone the chance to be a friend.

7

Step V: Examine Your Alternatives to the Behavior That's Causing the Problem

FRAN was such a sunny person that others basked in her warmth and humor. It would be impossible to distinguish between her looks and her aura, but I think she must have been pretty, too. It really didn't matter, because she carried with her such a sense of aliveness and fun. I was quite puzzled when she came to see me.

In describing her life, she deepened my puzzlement by enumerating the obvious satisfactions in it. Her husband was a graphic designer who shared her love for their two small children and spent a lot of time with his family. Fran's face lit up when she mentioned him—no problem there. The children were healthy and bright; Fran enjoyed them thoroughly. No problem there. Finally I asked her what she wanted to achieve in therapy.

"That's just it, I don't know. I have a wonderful life. I love being with my husband and children." She sighed—the deep kind of sigh that always seems to punctuate the sentences of depressed patients. With Fran, the sigh was more like a haze spread over her sunniness.

"Is this all life's about for me, Dr. Greenwald? *Is* this all there is? I go to parties, and the women are mothers and have careers too, and I feel like a little brown hen. I know I could be doing more, I just don't know if I want to, or what it might be, or even if I should do more. I couldn't be more confused—and I'm not used to being confused. It's just that all these questions have gotten trapped in my mind and I can't get rid of them or shut them up. It just doesn't seem to be enough, any more, being just a housewife."

"Is it enough for you?" I asked her. "Let's find out."

We talked about Fran's childhood, which had been happy, particularly as she had been her father's favorite. He had always treated her as an equal, discussing his law cases with her and listening to her opinion. She felt she had a good legal mind and assumed she would become a lawyer like him. Instead she had fallen in love and gotten married right after graduating from college.

To her surprise Fran found a real vocation in mothering, experiencing it as deeply satisfying and a constant challenge to her imagination. She was fascinated by her children and their friends; she gave them her full attention and they responded by opening up to her. They told her things most adults don't take time to listen to—their questions, their dreams, their fears. She listened closely and gave appropriate responses. (They must have been appropriate, because her circle of small friends kept growing.)

I was intrigued by her reports of various conversations with children. "You know," I said, "it strikes me that you are a brilliant friend to these children, including your own. What a mother! It's interesting, you know—we don't hear people evaluate mothering as anything other than good or bad. It's clear to me that you have a rare gift."

She responded by trying to make *me* feel better. She assured me that she did understand intellectually that she was a rare mother, and appreciated my having recognized her talent. Yet a few sessions later she still felt down. The nagging discontent just wouldn't go away.

"So maybe you do want to have a career as well. You're obviously smart and energetic enough to add one to your other responsibilities."

I asked Fran to close her eyes and imagine herself as a psychiatrist, getting up and going into an office, listening to other people's problems morning to night. She was very imaginative at describing herself in such a life. Seeing patients and writing papers, going to conferences and addressing large audiences as an innovator in child psychiatry, traveling all over the world as a guest lecturer.

"How do you feel about all of that?" I asked her.

"Well, I can see that I have a great deal to contribute. I love the attention and the excitement of exchanging ideas, but most of the time I am wondering what Larry and Patricia are doing. I think I have all that attention already, on a smaller scale. And I really do exchange ideas with the children and my husband. And they need *my* attention right now, more than I need a career—I can always have a career when they reach college. I guess the important thing right now is that I want to give my attention to them. It's my choice, isn't it?"

I knew better than to let her drop the subject too fast. We went through every career she had ever considered—ballerina, lawyer, actress, executive. She tried them all out in her mind. She enjoyed the challenge of each career, and she considered carefully the advantages of each and the demands on her time that would come out of the time she now spent with her family. As she put each dream to rest, Fran became more and more comfortable with her choice.

Her mild depression, her discontent, really had come about from her not having mourned all the dreams that had died. These dreams had become increasingly disturbing as Fran got older, until she acknowledged their importance and put them to rest. Then, when people asked her what she did, she answered "a lot"—and proceeded to tell them about it. She was probably as entertaining on the subject of her life as the other people were about theirs.

Some weeks later Fran reported with pleasure an incident that made her realize just how happy she was. She had visited an old friend of hers who was a successful actress. She brought along her children, who enchanted her friend. As Fran left, she saw the actress, who was not married, look longingly at Fran and the children—"Just the way I look at her picture when she opens in a new play. The thing is, I know her well enough to know that she's really happy and satisfied in her career. What I saw on her face that night backstage was just a little moment of mourning."

Depression most often comes in like a fog and obscures everything—at least, it has reached that point by the time most patients seek me out for help. Fortunately for Fran, her perceptions were usually so clear that even a slight haze disturbed her enough to take action. She simply could not deny for long the drain that her dreams and demands made on her energy and attention.

Fran was such an honest person that she did not try to keep her dreams alive by talking about how she really must get around to studying law, or assuring her friends that she could have been a prima ballerina. Instead, she came to me and consciously examined each of these dreams, experiencing the loss of rejecting each one—and, consequently, the satisfaction of the choice she *had* made.

To put it another way, until she came to me Fran had not given herself the listening, the attention that she lavished on her husband and children.

Many people would accept Fran's low-level depression as the price one pays for a basically happy life. But Fran sensed that without the deadening twinges of discontent she would have more of herself to give—and get back. Instead of seeing herself as a victim, she got help in looking at her alternatives. "Choose the happy alternative." In Fran's case, the happy alternative turned out to be the one she'd chosen.

Many of us try to avoid responsibility for ourselves and our lives, and all of us at times have a wish to evade it. One great way of avoiding responsibility is to tell ourselves that there is no other choice—then we can remain victims.

We're victims of a tyrannical husband or a devouring wife, of our workaholic bosses or the societal pressure to achieve. Or we're victims of our unhappy childhoods. It can even get worse: What about our genes? What can we do about *them*? We're victims, that's all. There's no hope.

I remember a woman I worked with in New York who, like nearly all the members of her family, was an alcoholic. *Un*like the other members of her family, Annie was (as she put it) a "recovering" alcoholic. We had lunch together from time to time, and one day she told me how hopeless she had felt when she was first getting sober. I asked her for details (I was interested, because Annie was one of the happiest women I knew).

"The worst time was a bitter gray day in January," she told me. "On Christmas Eve my husband had left me with my six-year-old daughter and his sixteen-year-old son by his first wife. I'd lost my job a month earlier, and I'd just come out of the hospital after almost dying of jaundice. All I wanted to do about any of these problems was drink, which my doctor had assured me would land me in the grave within two years.

"I went to Alcoholics Anonymous with no real hope but a lot of desperation, and after a week or so of meetings I asked a wonderful, flaky woman—she reminded me of Gracie Allen—to be my AA sponsor. She'd been sober eight years and she was truly wise, but everything she said came out funny, just a little off. Maybe that's why I listened to her—I kept hearing such unexpected things, and I've always loved surprises.

"Anyway, that morning in January I woke up and felt totally overwhelmed, before I even got out of bed. I didn't, however, feel totally alone—I called my sponsor and told her how down I was. 'I know taking a drink would just make every problem I have so

much worse,' I said, 'and I really hate feeling so sorry for myself.
But all of you keep saying how important it is to talk about what's
bothering us, so . . .'

"'It sounds like everything is bothering you,' she said. 'I think
you have a lot of things to feel sorry for yourself about. So go with
it. Don't even get out of bed, just lie there and deliberately remind
yourself of every single reason you can think of to feel sorry for
yourself. But set a time limit—use an alarm clock if you have to,
but cut yourself off after half an hour. Let's see . . . it's ten o'clock.
I'm going to hang up now, and you call me back at ten-thirty.'

"It sounded like the nuttiest advice I'd ever heard in my life—but
what could I expect from a woman who reread James Thurber
whenever she was feeling loosely wrapped? I didn't set the alarm,
but I kept an eye on my bedside clock as I dragged out every
problem in my life at the moment.

"It was a perfect orgy of self-pity, let me tell you. My husband,
whom I still loved, was never coming back, and I didn't have any
money and didn't have a job, and I was going to have to divorce the
husband and I didn't even have a lawyer, and how could I possibly
get through a divorce without picking up a drink? My little girl was
thoroughly confused, my stepson was stoned on grass all the
time—and the vacuum cleaner didn't work. With a husband who'd
left me and a stepson who was always stoned, how was I ever going
to take care of things like broken vacuum cleaners?

"I cried and I felt hopeless and I cried some more. Then, after
about twenty minutes, I began to feel a little strange—as if there
were bubbles inside me, and the bubbles were moving up through
my body. I was trying to think of another problem to cry over, and
another voice in my head was saying things like, 'A month ago you
were nearly dead and now you're alive, your daughter was sick
with worry and now she's just confused, you weren't just unem-
ployed you were unemployable. Most of all, you had to have a
drink every four hours or so and now you don't. Life is just one
broken vacuum cleaner after another—and so what?'

"The thought of the vacuum cleaner really did it. I started to giggle a little bit, then some more, until finally I was laughing, this great shout of laughter was breaking all round me and filling up my life . . .

"I felt *very* silly—and very glad to be alive. And in the five years since then I've had many things to be sad about—the saddest was when my sponsor died this year—but I've never completely lost that feeling of being glad I'm here, and I've never had to take a drink.

"I don't watch a clock any more, but I still let myself be with my own awful feelings when they come. I'm always amazed at how quickly they break up into bubbles of laughter, letting me see what's funny about what's making me sad. Usually what's funny is the way I overdramatize the problem."

We take ourselves so seriously. Every day it's open-heart surgery, and to kill the pain or blot out the anxiety we reach for the drink, the drug, the food—or the drama. Instead of experiencing our suffering, as Annie learned to do, we dramatize it and surround it with so many justifications that it's all but impossible to get rid of. We're also likely to become too involved in the drama to realize our alternatives, particularly the ones that would rob us of the victim role.

Choosing to be a victim is, of course, one of the alternatives available to us. As an old man in a mental health clinic said, "Aw, let me alone, Doc. All I got is my misery, and you want to take that away, too?"

Choosing not to choose, not to decide, is yet another alternative. Carol, a shy and unassertive housewife, was miserable because her husband was cold and abusive. Her mother and sister were constantly urging her to leave him, which only made her more miserable. She was too frightened to move out on her own, having married the man in the first place to escape her bossy mother and pushy sister. "I don't know what to do," she said. "I can't decide."

Sometimes it may not be appropriate to make a decision, no matter how pressured you feel. When I told Carol that she could decide not to decide at the moment, that such a serious decision ought not to be forced, she was relieved. "You'll know when you're ready to decide," I told her.

"When?"

"When you make the decision. Until then, you're not ready. For now, you can just look at all the ways you might handle the situation. Don't push yourself."

Lucille was a lady wrestler who came to see me convinced that no happy alternative was available to her. She had hugged her latest boyfriend and broken his ribs. "I'm extremely passionate," she told me. "And I can't help it that I'm so strong—I'm a wrestler. This always happens to me. I just get carried away. I really don't have any choice, and I really hate being lonely."

"How many ribs have you broken, Lucille?"

"Lots."

It turned out that Lucille was only ordinarily passionate. But she was extraordinarily angry. She'd gotten very little attention from the opposite sex when she was younger; she was big for her age and not particularly attractive. Her first dating relationships ended badly. Two boys dropped her in succession, and Lucille made an operative decision: I'll show them. By the time she had attained success in her chosen profession, she had the means to crush them.

So many of us overgeneralize from our experience. One woman has let us down, so women will always let you down. One man has hurt us, so that's what men do, they hurt you. Lucille got dropped and then proceeded to ensure that she would get revenge before she got dropped: she broke her boyfriends' ribs.

Now it's hard to see a wrestler as a victim, but that's exactly how Lucille saw herself when she began psychotherapy. Once she became aware of how angry she was, she soon became aware of her alternatives: break their ribs or don't break their ribs.

Her overall situation didn't change—she was still not particularly attractive. That, of course, doesn't necessarily determine whether or not the opposite sex is interested in you. Men still offered Lucille their ribs—to embrace or break, as she chose. Once she could see that if she didn't hurt them, they might not hurt her, her boyfriends were a lot safer and Lucille was a lot less lonely.

Some people would consider Lucille fortunate. She really had only two alternatives, and one was a happy one. A lot of people are convinced that they only have two alternatives and both are intolerable. Some along these lines: "Shall I kill him, or shall I kill myself?"

This life-or-death approach is by no means limited to dilemmas of serious proportions. "Shall I finish this book on happiness or commit suicide?" Well, I didn't really consider suicide, but I've heard dilemmas couched in those terms so often that urgent problems often take that form in my mind—so I can get my own attention. Writing has always involved a certain amount of agonizing decision on my part.

When Theodore Reik was alive I had a running conversation with him about writing that lasted for years. Once I told him I was blocked and he quoted Thomas Mann: "A professional writer is a person who doesn't like to write." That made me feel a little better, but it didn't help me with the book I was working on. I told him so the next time I saw him, and he went biblical on me: "Even God rested on the seventh day," he said. (Reik also loved to speak in parables, a useful way to communicate because the recipient has to work to understand what is meant.)

This one I really thought about. For me the exciting part of writing had always been thinking up the ideas. *That* was godlike. I had a wonderful idea—but then I had to work. I did not feel godlike at all when it came down to the tedious, demanding task of actually organizing my material, elaborating on my ideas, writing and rewriting. Naturally my demand on myself—that I be a genius—ensured that the words never equaled the idea.

A few years later I met Reik on the street, and he asked me how the writing was going. (He was convinced that I was a writer, so I never minded his asking.) I was agonizing, as usual, so I asked him how on earth he had ever managed to write thirty-nine books. This time he didn't quote anybody or drag God into it. "I force myself," he said.

In other words, he had made a decision to force himself to write. He did explain that the more he forced himself, the easier the writing process became. This time I was able to use his advice in completing the book I was working on. The more I challenged my fear of committing myself to paper, the less it frightened me— writing *that* book. Unfortunately I discovered that such fears do not disappear permanently. They can become as unmanageable as ever when I start a new book.

The point is, some problems we face have to be faced over and over, and the way we solve them from year to year doesn't have to be the same. When it came to writing this book, as I said, I decided not to force myself. Having a co-author is a different experience that has opened up a whole new set of alternatives for me. Now when I think about writing another book, I don't get that sinking feeling that agony is right around the corner. A good time seems right around the corner—I find that I enjoy collaboration enormously. For now, this is an alternative I'm happy with. Who knows how I'll feel in another few years? I look forward to finding out.

One of the techniques I use with my patients is to give them choices about everything conceivable—whether or not to sit up or lie on the couch, open the window, discuss their dreams, put on the air conditioner, or take off a jacket. I get them used to the fact that their decisions matter—and, at the same time, that their decisions are no big deal.

I also tell them there are many ways of conducting therapy. I ask them to tell me how I can help them. I say—and mean it—that they know what's best for them. Even if they choose to let *me* choose, I point out that not making a choice is a form of decision, too.

What I want to establish is an atmosphere of trust, a "no-lose" situation. People so often go for help because they're convinced they are in a no-win situation. Many of us feel that we're walking through the shellfire of "shoulds" shot at us by family, bosses, friends, and society—and when that's not happening we are being sentenced by the judge. It's really a wonder that we can hear ourselves well enough to make anything but the most fundamental decisions.

I think we should take all the time we want, or need. After all, the future course of history will not be affected by my decision. Sometimes when I have a decision to make, I make a game out of finding alternatives. I also do this with patients, and we often laugh a lot together—which is a pleasant change from agonizing. We think of outrageous possibilities. (A woman doesn't have to be a wrestler to come up with a bizarre fantasy for revenge on the man in her life.)

Sometimes I carry out an outrageous act, myself. I had a patient once who wouldn't talk—at all, not just in therapy. Stella had dummied up on her husband; her silence was driving him crazy, so he brought her to me. Eventually I learned that when she was little she had decided to deal with her anger and fear by switching off her response mechanisms. Her family had been overwhelmingly loud and frightening when Stella made the slightest comment, so she pretty much gave up talking. Predictably, she married a man who overreacted to things just the way her family had.

This I found out much later. Because, at first, Stella wouldn't talk to *me,* either. After giving monosyllabic responses to my questions (in between long, long silences), she finally explained that the only time she felt free to speak up as a child was if she crawled under the table and talked while they were eating.

I asked Stella if she would feel more comfortable getting under the big desk in my office. She just shook her head, so I said, "Okay, *I'll* get under." So I crawled under my desk and we had a pretty good dialogue for the rest of the session.

When she came back the next week, she wasn't talking again. I got up from my chair and started to get under the desk, and she said, "I'll talk, I'll talk! Just don't get under that goddamn desk again!" She didn't have any trouble talking to me from then on. Sometimes these outrageous decisions pay off for me, but sometimes there are repercussions. Her husband called me and said, "My wife is beginning to hallucinate. Do you know what she told me happened in your office?"

After her husband's reaction to my under-the-desk therapy, Stella and I spent some of our time together laughing. We would practice finding the comic aspects in all the situations that froze her into silence. When you're laughing you are not silent. And laughter is a pleasant antidote to anger.

If you have really paid attention to the Direct Decision Therapy steps, and worked on them, and still can't see your alternatives—stop thinking about it for a while. Go on to something else, just drop it. I have had patients who stopped coming to me, just as depressed, just as compulsive as they were when they began therapy. Then, months later, I have come across them and found that they are like different people. The problems have cleared up, and they either tell me they're happy or their satisfaction is so obvious they don't need to tell me.

Things can work out better sometimes when we leave them alone for a while. Once you do decide to examine your alternatives, give yourself enough time to relax with them—even have some fun with them. After all, you're only going to *try* something different, or try it on for size, or perhaps not try it at all. There's no deadline, no contract, no Faustian bargain to worry about.

Remember, there is no evidence that any therapy makes you a better person. But there is plenty of evidence that not beating up on yourself will make you a happier person. So if acting as your own therapist sets off a tirade from the judge, go watch Woody Allen, or the Marx Brothers, or "Candid Camera" reruns—anything that amuses you. I think a good laugh will make you a better person.

Step V: Examine Your Alternatives to the Behavior That's Causing the Problem

- Think of a piece of parental advice that was good for you.

- Aside from salary, add up the payoffs your job gives you.

- Think of a person you like whom you used to despise.

- Think of one bad habit and imagine getting along without it.

- Try or recall—or imagine—what your parents were like when they were your age.

- Ask yourself whether your children resemble you at the same age.

- Think of as many ways as you can in which you are different at home and at work.

- Consider whether you like yourself best the way you are at home or the way you are at work.

- Decide to switch some of these ways from home to work, or vice versa.

- Consider what career you would choose if you were to start over.

- Think about what really keeps you in your career.

- Think about what's really stopping you from changing careers.

- Consider what you'd get out of going to school.

- Think of what subject you'd like to pursue if you took a course.

- Consider what kind of education you're getting, non-academically speaking.

- Think of all the qualities that charmed you about your spouse or lover when you first met.

- Remember what charmed your spouse or lover when you first met.

- Ask yourself what qualities you'd most like in a spouse or lover.

- Think about what your life would be like if you were really on your own.

- Think about what your life would be like if you shared it with someone.

- Consider what's satisfying about your life that depends only upon you.

8

Step VI: Choose Your Alternative and Decide to Put It into Practice

WHEN I first saw Helen, I immediately thought of those earthquake victims you see on television. And listening to this small, plain, gray-haired woman in her fifties, I could understand her state of devastation. Her entire world had collapsed, and without so much as a rumble of warning.

"Since Michael moved out I walk around the house surrounded with everything we shared for over twenty years," she said, "and I still can't believe this has happened. I don't know whether it feels more like he has died, or I've died. I'm a ghost haunting my own house."

Michael, a prominent physician, had married Helen when she was a nurse and he a student in medical school. Helen supported him through his career—financially at first, then as helpmeet, homemaker, hostess, and mother to their three children. He relied on her to manage all of these areas of their life, and Helen managed not only expertly but with a genuine sense of satisfaction. She had been a woman people looked up to, not just because Michael was such a successful doctor but also because Helen was the epitome of the doctor's wife.

"I really was very good at what I did," she told me. "But it's hard to be the perfect doctor's wife if you don't have the doctor."

Her eyes snapped into focus as I let out a little chuckle over this observation. I smiled and was glad to see her smile back although I could see her wondering why either one of us was smiling.

"I know what you've told me is nothing to smile about," I said, "in fact it's a very tough situation. But I think there's a lot more to you, and I want to hear it."

As Helen talked, it occurred to me that her situation is practically epidemic among professionals: the man becomes successful and, along with the Mercedes, acquires a younger woman—abandoning his wife. When this happens it is nearly always viewed as a catastrophe, which is certainly the way Helen saw it at first. And at first, when I saw women like Helen, I tended to share their feeling of hopelessness. What could an ordinary woman in her fifties do, totally unprepared to see herself as anything other than Mrs. Dr. So-and-So?

I learned, however, that if a woman like Helen begins to see herself as an individual, she often finds out that what made her enjoy her roles as wife and mother so much was her capacity for enjoyment—not, narrowly speaking, the family that happened to be lucky enough to have her. Once a woman begins to see herself *as* herself, a great deal begins to happen. Helen, for example, turned out to be an extraordinary "ordinary" woman, surprising me constantly with her capacity for humor and her resiliency.

"I'm rather a conservative person," she told me that morning, glancing down at her well-made skirt and silk blouse. "Now wouldn't I look foolish as a cowgirl or a gypsy? Well, a few months ago Michael started dressing like our daughter's boyfriends. Then he started dating girls younger than our daughter." A look of disbelief crossed her face. "I told him he couldn't do that, and he just moved out. He's living with this young woman right now . . ."

"So what do *you* want to do? Continue to haunt the house?"

"No. But what can I do? And who would want me?"

"You tell me."

She looked surprised at this approach, but she took a deep breath and went on.

"Well, I could go back to nursing. Yes, I could, I was an excellent nurse. Maybe it's sour grapes, but I think I may have liked it more than I liked being a doctor's wife."

"Good, that's settled. I believe you. Now what else?"

"Well . . . This is hard for me to say, but I know I'm not a bit glamorous or even youthful. I don't think any men would be interested in someone like me these days."

"If you say so."

"You mean only if I say so?" She was very smart.

"Look," I said, "there's one thing I've had proven from experience and observation, over and over again. It doesn't matter whether you're fat or thin, young or old, beautiful or ugly—none of that makes much difference. Attraction seems to depend on an attitude, or Russian roulette, or the Good Fairy, but what you look like isn't what it depends on."

"That's hard for me to believe—about myself, that is. But you know, I have been noticing men and women down at the marina shopping center, and I think you may be right. I'll just let me be for a while, then."

It wasn't long before Helen was showing up for her sessions full of exciting plans.

"I've sold that old mausoleum. I'm tired of rattling around in it. I'm going to find a cozy apartment looking over the water—and I can do it up just the way I want it. My bedroom is going to be full of all the flowers and airy-fairy things Michael never would stand for.

"You know, every day there's a voice inside me that gets a little louder. I start to do something—buy something in the supermarket, say—and the voice says, 'Helen you never liked that. Put that back!' Sometimes the voice makes me jump and I actually look around to see if anyone else has heard it. And sometimes I

answer back, out loud. I say, 'You're right, I'm not going to buy it.'
I get some very peculiar looks.

"So what? More and more, lately, I just don't care if anyone
hears me or not. I'm so happy to hear that voice. It's as if I'm
getting to know myself for the first time in my life."

Helen had a good time getting to know herself. She kept to her
conservative style of dressing, but she chose brighter, prettier
colors. Years seemed to have dropped off her face; her look was
softer and livelier. She started studying for an advanced nursing
degree and took her pick from several good job offers when she
finished.

Her circle of friends changed as she listened more and more to
the voice of Helen. She told me about her new friends, friends she
had picked simply because they interested her. "And you know
something, Dr. Greenwald? They like *me* for me, too."

One day she came into my office with her arm in a cast. "Well,
you'll never believe it, but all my life I've wanted to learn to roller
skate, and nowadays everyone seems to be skating. So I bought
myself some skates and went to a rink to find someone to teach
me."

"How did you hurt your arm?"

"They really are the most beautiful skates, red leather with silver
laces. I found out I'm not bad, I learned to stand and turn in five
minutes. I was doing just fine, when some kids started fooling
around, and one came barrelling into me backward. Over I went
and fell just the wrong way on my wrist. I have another lesson this
week, though. Fortunately you use legs and not arms to skate
with."

I told Helen that I had always wanted to learn body surfing, and
that she and her roller skates were an inspiration. They were, too. I
went out and tried surfing.

Helen's confidence and singularity served as inspiration to her
daughter, who had been drifting along not at all sure what she

wanted to do with her life. Not long after her mother's metamorphosis, she decided to enter medical school—not just because
her father was a doctor, but because she realized how much she
wanted to go into medicine and how important it was to do what
you want with your life.

By the time a year had gone by, Helen had two men interested in
her. She felt no necessity to choose between them—and, in fact,
had relatively little time available to spend with either one. She was
too busy with her studies and other activities.

"Who would have thought it? Here I am, turning down dates
because I have to study. And I met Michael in the supermarket the
other day—I haven't seen him for so long. I hate to say this, but he
just looks silly, dressing like that. And all he could talk about was
his hair transplants."

Helen had suffered a real and humiliating loss—abandonment
by the person she most loved and trusted. Some people never
recover from such a blow to their sense of self. They spend the rest
of their lives suffering. Or scheming (consciously or not) to get
back at the person who dealt the blow.

The trouble is, like Candice's mother, the culprits usually don't
even notice—much less suffer. The suffering can even become its
own reward, the big payoff: if we stop, we would also have to
forgive the people who caused our suffering, *and we want to make
them pay.* And so we offer ourselves as perpetual sacrifices, as a
reminder of a parent's mistakes, of a husband's or wife's desertion,
of a child's ingratitude. . . .

Helen had terrific material for membership in the saddest-story-
ever-told club, but she chose not to join. Her decisions to change
were frightening as well as thrilling, and she did not initially see
herself as the kind of person who does frightening, thrilling things.
Her payoff, of course, was terrific: she got herself.

Some of my patients never make a decision consciously, thus

never allow themselves the kind of freedom that Helen found. They don't realize that never making a decision of one's own is in itself a decision—the decision not to decide.

Then there are others who always let other people decide for them. That way no one can blame them if anything goes wrong— or, better yet, they can blame the decision maker if anything goes wrong. They get to feel superior, without acknowledging that they threw the burden of choice on someone else's shoulders.

Remember Paul, the passive-aggressive who was driving Alice crazy with his refusal to participate in any decisions? At one point I confronted him with a challenge, one I had used successfully in the past with patients who are afraid of murderous anger. I asked Paul to make a decision that he would never kill anyone. He was surprised—so accustomed to his mild-mannered act that he'd almost convinced himself.

"I'm serious," I told him. "I want you to promise me seriously that you will never kill anyone. You see, if you make a conscious decision not to kill anyone, maybe you can allow yourself to express some of your anger safely. You won't have to be worried about killing any more—and you won't have to go on burning up inside, either."

Paul looked puzzled and thoughtful.

"That goes for you, too," I said. "Promise not to kill yourself."

Now he looked alarmed—and angry.

"Don't worry, I don't think you're suicidal. It's just that you have no practice expressing any strong emotions directly. I want everyone covered in this agreement. Then no one has to worry about being the object of your anger—including yourself."

It took Paul two sessions before he got up the courage to agree to the promise. What he did was to replace his old life decision about anger with a new one prohibiting murder. He was fully aware that things were going to change for him after his decision, which was why he took so long to make it.

He did begin to express many emotions directly, not just anger. He began asserting himself with Alice, which at first created a whole new set of problems. "You've ruined our marriage," she said to me on the phone soon after. Paul also began changing his style at work, which caused some seismic tremors there. His co-workers had no experience of a Paul who said what he wanted or disagreed with anyone. His policy of noninvolvement had spoiled the people in his life.

I told Alice, "You made him come to group for this very reason. Now you don't want him to have opinions?"

"If I'd known his opinions would be so different from mine I never would have started all of this. I want him back the way he was. All we do now is talk, talk, talk."

"Well, you have to admit it's more interesting than being furious all the time."

Alice started to come to another group herself, to help her deal with her husband's new personality—"my Frankenstein's monster," she called it. Alice was experiencing the truth of that old adage: Be careful what you wish for, lest you get it. (Which is one of the reasons I never insist on decisions for change.)

Remember Peter, the sufferer? He never felt completely safe not suffering. Once he recognized his life decision, he was able to let it go more often. But the minute he felt threatened, out would come the suffering number. The difference was that when his family called him on his act, he admitted it—even when he didn't stop it. "Well, you know what a sufferer I am . . . Oh, my god, what am I going to do?"

And his decision to suffer didn't have such a detrimental effect on his family any more. They were able to treat it with some humor, and Peter accepted their teasing with "suffering" good grace.

Peter was someone I was able to reach through his suppressed sense of humor. Little by little we were able to diminish his inhibition against being funny. At first he would say, "What's there to be funny about?" Finally he realized that he was really saying, "If I'm funny, nobody will know I'm suffering." Which, of course, he had decided long ago to make abundantly clear at every opportunity possible. A whole new world opened up for Pete when he was able to see that he could be funny *and* suffer.

Since people come to me in such times of trouble, I'm delighted when I detect the seeds of humor buried in their sad tales. Like Helen, who seemed hopeless until—quite seriously—she started describing her life in terms that made me want to smile. The smile, of course, was no accident. She turned out to have a wonderful sense of humor, a sense of fun in life. I simply encouraged it and used it with her until those parts of herself she began listening to seriously were the spontaneous, naturally happy parts.

Sometimes a patient will feel he shouldn't bring humor "in here," as therapy must be serious business. But the point, surely, is not seriousness versus humor. That's the wrong equation. What such a patient really means is *grimness* versus humor. Now, we all have serious problems, but we don't have to be grim about them. Some people feel, "No one will take me seriously if I laugh." Not true. Some things are so serious that you had better laugh.

The point is this: even if you decide to stay exactly the way you are, I will feel I have done you (and the world) a favor if I can convince you that life is not so grim that you can't laugh. If you can laugh, then you can be happy—at least some of the time.

I love proofs that Direct Decision Therapy works on all levels of daily living, including the less serious ones. My co-author wrote me about such an instance, adding that she thought it showed the "infectious" nature of the therapy:

"I was in a wonderful mood when I got back from California

after working with you. I decided to take a cab from the terminal to the long-term parking lot. The driver gunned the engine as he left the terminal, only to slam on his brakes because the traffic on the access road was so slow. 'Why did you have to get me, lady? They got buses to the lots, why don't you leave us cabbies alone . . . ?' On and on.

"I sank lower in my seat, a little frightened but also indignant. 'He's spoiling my wonderful mood. This is his job and I'm paying him to insult me?' 'Wait a minute,' another voice in my head said. '*Listen* to him.'

"I listened. 'Look at this traffic, I wait in line two hours for this lousy fare, now look what I have to get back into just to get to the line again.' I looked at the traffic. He was right. My saving ten minutes had cost him an hour.

"We were almost at the parking lot. I reached over the back of his seat with a five-dollar bill and said, 'I'd take a bus now if I could start all over again—I see what you're up against. Please keep the change, and accept my apology.'

"He took a deep breath, and when he spoke his tone wasn't snarly, just a little glum. 'Oh, you gotta get where you're going to. You got a right to take a taxi if you want.' I said, 'I know, but when I've taxied to the lot before, it's been earlier and there's no traffic. Next time I'll look first.' 'Aw, how could you know, you're probably tired from working.' 'Well, I just want you to know I don't enjoy making people suffer and I wish you didn't have to backtrack through all that traffic.'

"We were at the parking lot by now, and he jumped out and opened my door. 'You know, lady, you're really a nice person. I'm glad I got you, I hope I get you all the time.' 'Well, I hope you feel that way when you're back in the line.'

"He drove off with a wave, and a man getting out of a car next to me said, 'What did you do for *him?*' I thought for a minute and then said, 'If you want to know the truth, I gave him a hard time. But in the end I guess he decided not to see it that way.'"

Suddenly there is a mountain of research on humor and brain chemicals and highs, some of which I have mentioned. The recent research on jokes (what kind you laugh at reveals what kind of personality you have) strikes me as a real fun killer. All I can see is people ingesting all that information and forcing laughter at what they consider the "right" kind of joke. And forcing a laugh seems to me a good way to turn laughter into work.

The recent research on smiles is more to my liking. I smiled the minute I saw the headline to an article in *The New York Times*: "Study Says Smile May Indeed Be an Umbrella." I quote:

> Just the act of flexing facial muscles into the character-
> istic expressions of joy or other emotions, the researchers
> found, can produce effects on the nervous system that
> normally go with these emotions . . . Dr. Paul Ekman, a
> psychologist at the University of California . . . believes
> the study shows the mechanics of facial-muscle move-
> ment are closely tied to the autonomic nervous system,
> which controls heart rate, breathing, and other vital
> functions.

So maybe the forced laugh or the forced smile set off the nervous system on the happy route, and then turn it into the real thing. So what do I know with my judgments about forced laughter!

The article went on to point out that the body produces different and appropriate sensations, the chemical responses to those facial expressions connected with six major emotions: anger, fear, disgust, surprise, sadness, and happiness. This is powerful ammunition for one of the oldest principles of modern psychology, the

James-Lange Theory, which says that we are happy because we laugh and sad because we cry. Out of this came the technique sometimes called "Act as if."

I have often suggested to depressed patients that they choose a way they would like to feel and then act that way. It works equally well for shy people, unassertive people, and bad-tempered people. I am happy to learn that there is even more evidence to support this technique, because it is such a simple one to follow. This new research suggests that it's even simpler than I thought it was: first rearrange your facial expression, then notice how you begin to feel and what you feel like doing.

Dr. Ekman also helped me directly by quoting (in the article) an excerpt from Edgar Allen Poe:

> In that work [the "Purloined Letter"], Poe wrote that when he wants to find out how wise, stupid, good or evil a character is or what he is thinking at the moment, "I fashion the expression of my face, as accurately as possible, in accordance with the expression of his, and then wait to see what thought or sentiments arise in my mind or heart."

As a therapist, I have found I can often understand how a person feels and even what he thinks by mirroring his expression or his bodily position.

It's nice to have your theories supported by scientific evidence. I've always had the theory that people can develop or find their sense of humor if they choose to. I've spoken in public many times on the subject, and I remember a man in the audience once who said, "I see I'll have to work at this." And I said, "No, you'll have to play with this."

That's another of my theories, that "play" gets us back to that spontaneous joy we experienced as children when we *were* playing. So often as adults we think we are playing when we're seriously involved in games. The difference between play and games, as I see it, is this: play is an attitude that makes activities pleasurable; games are bound by rules. Unfortunately, the "attitude rule" that goes with most games is, "Don't fool around, this is serious."

Play allows us to approach life's experiences looking for—and therefore finding—the lighter side. Aided by the buoyancy of a playful spirit, solutions and inspirations can float in on the tide of expectancy. The truly recreative benefit of play is to give us a playful spirit in the process of daily living, in our encounters with people and problems, so that like children (making faces and having fun) we can recapture the joy in living. We all can make faces if we want to. And, if we want to, we can have fun.

An attitude of play can make an enormous difference when it comes to choosing an alternative. The whole business of making decisions can get put into the category of demands, if we're not careful. I can just hear the judge: "Look, stupid, all of life is a decision. So pay attention, get serious, take responsibility for your decisions—you got nobody to blame but yourself!"

I'm here to tell your judge (and mine) that this attitude is the most likely to result in a damaging decision. I think you have a better chance of making the right decision if you play with it.

Here's a story Theodor Reik told me about Freud: Reik met Freud in the street one day just at the time Reik was trying to decide whether to get a Ph.D. in psychology or go to medical school so he could qualify as a psychiatrist. He was glad to run into Freud, who he was sure would have the last word on the pros and cons of lay analysis. I love Freud's advice: "Anything that important, don't think about. Do what you feel like doing."

When I think back on my own decisions, the truly satisfying

ones often "felt right" before I made them. Freud was really saying, "trust yourself," a piece of advice so wise that it has existed in various forms for thousands of years.

I know that sometimes it isn't so easy to stop worrying about an important decision, stacking up the pros and cons—and all the time the judge is racing out of his chambers to admonish you until you feel so pressured that all you can conclude is you don't know what to do. At times like this, here's what *I* do: I stop thinking about it. I consciously decide to postpone it for a while. I trust myself: the decision will materialize when all my subconscious forces have worked it over.

When things feel "right," your whole body (this includes your facial expressions) no longer resists making a decision. I've noticed that's when I get the strength to take risks, to challenge something I think needs challenging. I immediately feel high, and once I get started, all of these good feelings keep stimulating me and I stimulate them. The chemical process and the process of engaging in the activity perpetuate each other. All I have to do is overcome the initial reluctance.

As I see it, this is all connected to the true joy of accomplishing. (Notice I didn't say "accomplishment," which is another kind of joy.) I'm talking about enjoying the process of writing, cleaning the house, roller skating—of doing whatever we are doing, *fully*.

Our society is goal-oriented, and many of us rob ourselves of half the pleasure in living by projecting ourselves into the future ("What's it going to be like when . . . ?") or plunging ourselves into the past ("It's not what it used to be . . ." "I was lousy then . . ."). We should all look in the mirror when we catch ourselves thinking this way. I have, and my expression was *not* one of satisfaction.

Satisfaction comes when we pay attention to what we're doing, when we enter into it fully. That's what happiness is all about, the way I see it. If we can make a decision about that (which doesn't involve *changing* what we're doing, notice), then we can understand what George Bernard Shaw meant when he wrote:

> This is the true joy in life, the being used for a purpose recognized by yourself as a mighty one. The being a force of nature instead of a feverish selfish little clot of ailments and grievances complaining that the world will not devote itself to making you happy. I am of the opinion that my life belongs to the whole community and as long as I live it is my privilege to do for it whatever I can. I want to be thoroughly used up when I die, for the harder I work the more I live. I rejoice in life for its own sake. Life is no brief candle to me. It is a sort of splendid torch which I've got hold of for the moment and I want to make it burn as brightly as possible before handing it on to future generations.

It really doesn't matter whether or not the rest of the world defines your purpose as a mighty one. (Only the judge will get hung up on that definition.) Considering all the misery out there, I think deciding to be as happy as you can constitutes a terrific contribution to the world.

Step VI: Choose Your Alternative and Decide to Put It into Practice

- Imagine being marooned on an island. Consider:
  —who you would want with you, and
  —who would be the happiest when you were rescued and came home.

- Do something silly to—or with—your spouse.

- Watch your children doing something silly, and join them.

- Next time your spouse, child, or friend gets face-to-face furious with you, mimic his/her facial expressions exactly and see what happens.

- Imagine how you might quit your job tomorrow—gracefully—if you wanted to.

- Imagine what kind of job you'd take if you changed fields.

- Imagine yourself taking a year off and what you would do with your time.

- Try to remember a time when you played a role and it really paid off.

- Think of a time when you spontaneously went off somewhere overnight.

- Imagine spontaneously going off somewhere tonight.

9

Step VII: Support Yourself in Carrying Out Your Decision

WE have met all kinds of decision makers in this book, including people who decide not to make decisions and people who always seem to make the wrong decisions. But what about those of us who make splendid, wise decisions—and then can't carry them out?

This is my most common problem. I'm always looking for ways to support myself in my decisions to be the most brilliant, wisest, freshest, most playful, most understanding, kindest, thinnest, happiest psychotherapist-author around. As you can imagine, these goals keep me very busy and a little confused at times. In supporting myself in being happy, I'll decide on ice cream . . . and there we are, back to the first step of Direct Decision Therapy again.

But I am happy to say that this is the last step: Support yourself in carrying out your decision or decisions. This process often involves moment-by-moment decisions to carry us through to realizing one major decision. The changing of operational decisions is doomed to failure if we don't allow ourselves any flexibility. The greatest obstacle we can set in front of us is this: "From now on . . . and forever."

Examine your decision. Say it's a manageable one. For me it might be wanting to lose ten pounds. Ten pounds is too much to think about, all at once. Already I'm discouraged, it makes me depressed. When I'm depressed, ice cream therapy is the quickest . . .

So I break down my decision into parts. What about losing *one* pound? Now narrow the diet to one day, forget about the rest. At the end of one day, I reexamine my decision and concentrate on the next day.

With some obsessions the time frame may have to be narrowed down to an hour, or even ten minutes—not unusual when the obsession is smoking. The point is this: the overwhelming desire to eat, smoke, drink, suffer, judge, or do whatever you have decided not to do, will pass *whether or not you satisfy it.* I promise that it will go away, satisfied or not, . . . and of course it will come back. Awareness of this fact makes it a lot easier for us to busy ourselves with something distracting when under temptation. We don't have to give in and become consumed by that small part of ourselves hell-bent on dominating our behavior. We don't have to be so serious about it.

Dividing our decisions into smaller, more manageable ones by the day, by the hour, or if need be by the moment allows us to strengthen ourselves during those times that we succeed. So if one hour out of twenty-four you fail, look and see why *you decided* to change the decision that hour. Give yourself the choice to remake your decision and continue. Forgive yourself if you are tempted to sink into discouragement and hopelessness.

On the other hand, pay attention to the rewards for carrying out your decision. If there don't seem to be any immediate payoffs for changing some behavior, then devise a system of rewards for yourself—even if that just involves taking the time to appreciate your strength in sticking to your decision. And don't be stingy with your praise, either. Making yourself feel good stimulates those good brain chemicals that make you feel happy. Then your happiness has the possibility of stimulating the same thing in other people—and so on, in a chain reaction.

One way of supporting yourself is to remember that no decision need be forever. If you have decided to give up suffering, and suddenly you have heart palpitations over the prospect, calm down. You can choose: when to suffer and when to be cheerful. Direct Decision Therapy is just a tool that can be used at any time to help clear the air, to let you see where you've been and see what your choices are about where you are going.

People rarely make a single decision to be happy. It may be the easiest way, but usually we arrive at the happy alternative through small decisions, sometimes so small that they are neither noticed nor remembered. But the more aware we can become of all these decisions, big and small, the better our chance to repeat the ones that bring us happiness, until they become a way of life.

One of the classic definitions of maturity, of being an adult, is having the ability to postpone gratification. You may well wonder what's wrong with instant gratification? If giving that up is what goes with being an adult, why would anyone choose to grow up except sufferers?

Maybe a better definition of maturity would be developing the ability to gratify yourself while supporting your long-term decisions. This means figuring out rewards that provoke pleasurable feelings all along the way to reaching your goals.

There can be a double message where rewards are concerned. We are not just rewarding ourselves, we're also giving ourselves permission to have pleasure—for a good reason, if we need a reason. An example would be the mother who almost never takes time for herself because she's so busy doing things for her children. I convince her that she'd be a better mother if she had more fun. I tell her she'll help her children become happier people by acting as a role model—knowing that the only way this woman can possibly enjoy herself is if she thinks it will benefit the children. But enjoyment is enjoyment, and any way you can sneak it in, it's positive reinforcement.

Figuring out rewards can provide an opportunity to exercise your ingenuity. A friend of mine who wanted to stop smoking found that she could deal with her craving for nicotine by paying single-minded attention to the person she was with whenever she felt the urge to light up. She tended to be a social smoker and found that when she concentrated absolutely on whomever she was with, she got a reward more satisfying than the cigarette would have been. Certainly this substitution expanded and deepened her enjoyment of other people—and paying attention isn't hazardous to your health.

This is an example of the well-established principle of substitution—as opposed to deprivation. And if you explore your own way of experiencing situations, as did my friend who stopped smoking, it could lead to a whole new and satisfying way of being with people. Or with yourself.

Friends can be an important source of help in carrying out a new decision. Sometimes, making a pact with a friend will create a public framework that strengthens your resolve. Friends can also give support when you are tempted not to stick to your decision. A phone call for help can be a constructive and often enjoyable distraction.

Of course, we all have friends far more willing to support our weaknesses than our strengths. Keep this in mind when you choose the friends whose support you want to enlist. If your neighbor starts baking cakes for you when you've asked her to support you in losing weight, don't bother to sort out her motives or behavior. Just stay out of her kitchen until you finish your diet. This is no time to complicate your life with other people's problems. (You could end up telling yourself that it's much more important to eat a piece of cake and help out your friend.)

Setting off a conflicting set of decisions can be averted by using more than one person—a fail-safe system, so to speak. Declaring your decision in front of friends and asking for their support has at least three possible benefits: (1) You may get terrific support from them—ideas, enthusiasm, etc. (It's always easier to help solve someone else's problem.) (2) You give them the opportunity to *be* supportive—or to ask for support themselves—and generate enthusiasm in achieving various goals. (3) Having made a commitment in front of them, you'll find it easier to stick to your decision. (It isn't just you who'll know if you slip.)

The oldest support group of all is the family. Unfortunately, not all families are supportive. But often a family that seems unsupportive can be looked at in another way. It's not a question (too many people think it *is*) of good guys and bad guys. As a family therapist, I look upon the family as a system whose goal is to learn to support each other. Difficulties arise when the group divides up and spends its time and energy blaming certain members for being the way they are.

The Blanchard family came to see me after Karen, the mother, had decided to go back to school. She needed support in carrying out this decision and was hurt when she got just the opposite. George, her husband, sneered at her choice of social work as a career. "The next thing I know she'll be going off to join the Peace Corps and abandon us altogether," he said. The three children couldn't seem to stop quarreling with each other. When they weren't engaged in combat, Karen said, "I think they spend all their extra time thinking up demands for me so they can all descend on me at once, the minute I walk in the door from class. I never have five minutes of peace."

During therapy sessions, it was helpful for all of them to express their feelings of abandonment and jealousy of each other's share of Karen's limited time. But none of this made any real difference until Josh, the ten-year-old, responded to a suggestion I threw out: "Suppose you think of something you want to do together as a family, something you all can enjoy."

Josh said, "Let's go fishing." Suddenly these people changed from warring factions into a cooperative group working out the details of a fishing holiday. The bad feelings between them evaporated for the moment, and so I was able to point out that they had just demonstrated (1) that they could be cooperative, and (2) that their difficulties came out of a fear that the closeness they had experienced in the past was gone forever. I pointed out that Karen's study demands actually gave them a chance to become even closer by thinking of ways to help her and each other.

Now the Blanchards' family circumstances didn't change. Karen was still going for her degree and not on hand much for the children. George didn't suddenly profess a new-found respect for social work as a profession (but he didn't sneer as much, either). What had happened was that Josh's wish for a family holiday uncovered the desire they all had for family closeness.

It allowed one of those teachable moments. When Josh said, "This is a lot more fun than fighting," I asked him if he could continue having fun by thinking of ways he could help his mother get As in her courses. He thought about it a minute and was able to see that her school problems weren't very different from his. The children all put their heads together to help their mother study and developed a vested interest in protecting her valuable study time (they planned to check out their success when her first grades came in).

Olivia, a basically happy friend of mine, got through the basically unhappy experience of divorce by enlisting the support of friends and a family member in an unusual way. The decision to divorce was made by Olivia, whose husband had, as she saw it, left her for his work. "If he had left me for another woman, I could see the whole thing in more human terms, but I keep asking myself how did I wind up married to a workaholic? A robot? I know, it doesn't matter. What *does* matter is that I get on with my life."

Olivia went through a short period of blaming herself for failure, calling her family and friends and rehashing her decision to end her marriage, the feelings of emptiness in her life—even though her husband, a workaholic, had been absent 90 percent of the time anyway. Then, having noticed that interest in her sad tale was wearing thin, she decided to enlist her friends' support in different, very specific ways.

She asked her sister Carla, a demon for organization, to help with her closets and bureaus ("I suddenly have a *lot* of extra space," Olivia explained). She invited her best friend, an interior decorator, to rearrange the furniture, move it around so that the apartment wouldn't look the same. "I don't want to walk in and see 'his' chair staring at me from the same old place," she said. And when a particularly attractive single friend announced her departure for a skiing weekend, Olivia asked if she might come along.

These people not only agreed to support Olivia in the ways she had asked; they also were delighted by her willingness to join them in enjoying themselves. Olivia knew the value of having fun. And the more she set up enjoyable circumstances, the more fun she and her supporters had.

This approach, she found, heals hurt much faster than sinking into a depression. "The whole experience taught me something really valuable," she said. "Instead of letting myself feel like a hopeless failure and making my friends and family feel helpless when they said, 'Is there anything I can do?' I decided to tell the truth. 'Yes, there is, and I'll tell you what.' It was a time when I really needed them, and I was lucky enough to have people who cared about me and wanted to help. My marriage was over, and I was still a lucky person."

What about people whose problems have distanced them from their family and friends, or whose problems call for help or expertise outside the reasonable limits of friendship and kinship? We are fortunate in the United States to have almost every kind of support group conceivable, from Alcoholics Anonymous and Gamblers Anonymous and Overeaters Anonymous to groups for families of the mentally ill to groups for single parents. Information about groups organized to support people with specific problems will be found in an appendix to this book.

I'm in favor of anything that works to help people be happy, and the help these groups offer can be invaluable. I realize that not everyone can allow himself to benefit from group support, but I have seen many skeptics' lives change as a result of one phone call made in a moment of desperation. Even a reluctant decision to get help can have wonderful payoffs.

Annie, my alcoholic friend who timed a self-pity orgy with an alarm clock in chapter 7, remembers vividly her negative reaction when someone suggested that she try Alcoholics Anonymous.

"My skin just crawled at the idea of sitting around in church basements with skid row bums and smelly, frowzy women. I was a lifelong nonjoiner—I quit Brownie Scouts at the age of ten and a marvelous job in my twenties just because it required weekly meetings."

Annie thought of herself at the time not as an alcoholic but as having a "drinking problem," which somehow seemed increasingly to elude her control. "The only reason I agreed to get help," she said, "was to get my mother to shut up. She was taking care of my little girl after I got out of the hospital, and she kept harping on A.A. until I told her, 'If you promise not to say another word about it, I'll go.' She shut up, and I went to my first meeting."

Annie was surprised at the variety of people she found in the meeting room. "Professional types, businessmen and women, people in work clothes and jeans and suits—even some teenagers who didn't look old enough to drink. Not at all what I'd expected.

A snappy looking woman with a wonderful laugh introduced herself and got me a cup of coffee."

"What struck me right away was how comfortable these people seemed with each other. *I* didn't feel comfortable—walking through those doors had been the hardest thing I'd done in years—but I did feel safe, somehow. I was just exhausted from keeping up a front, acting as though I was okay when I knew inside I was falling apart. And the huge problem I was trying to keep a secret from everybody, expecially myself, was exactly what made me acceptable in this group.

"The woman who'd brought me my coffee told me I didn't have to say I was an alcoholic. 'Just listen and see if anything you hear rings a bell,' she said. 'Maybe you're an alcoholic, maybe you're not—only you can decide.'

"Somehow, knowing I didn't have to identify myself as an alcoholic, pushed my 'contrary' button, and when the introductions were going around I actually heard myself say, 'My name is Annie, and I'm an alcoholic.' But even more shocking than hearing those words come out of my mouth was the sense of relief I felt. Everybody had been on my case for so long about my drinking, and here was a whole room full of people who found 'alcoholic' a perfectly acceptable thing to be. There was no judgment in anyone's eyes or voice. Against *my* preconceived judgments, I found myself liking these people."

Annie has been sober for six years now. She has shared with me valuable information about the function of support groups—especially the way they continue to function in a member's life even after the behavior that brought the person into the group has changed.

"I no longer have a drinking problem," she said. "That is, I never think of a drink as a solution to anything. But I'm still an alcoholic, and I can see now that what A.A. offered me wasn't just a way to stop drinking, but a way to start really living. I keep on learning ways to cope with my problems and enjoy my life and myself—from so very many people, so very much like me.

"What's even more important is that staying active in A.A. gives me the chance to help newcomers the way I was helped when I first came in. So I go to meetings, and I sponsor newcomers, and I go out speaking when I'm asked, and I use the twelve recovery steps in my life as best I can.

"And I do all this because it helps me—because it does the same thing for me that drinking used to do in the days before it became a problem: it makes me feel better.

"I've changed not just from drunk to sober, but from trapped to free. Those twelve steps are clearly set forth as *suggested* steps, and only the first one even mentions alcohol. The other eleven have to do with accepting ourselves and others the way we are. There's so much more room for growth and enjoyment when no one is forcing us to get help or to change."

My own philosophic leaning has always been toward letting people be, letting them decide in their own good time what they want out of life—including help, support, or happiness. (Perhaps this is because my personality resists with a vengeance control imposed from the outside.) The voluntary nature of the support offered by A.A. and other groups modeled after it has, I'm convinced, a lot to do with their success. The other success factor that strikes me with particular force is that of helping others by helping oneself. From my university days, I have never forgotten Alfred Adler's suggestion that a patient could cure his depression in seven days by thinking of something to do each day for a family member or friend that would really make a difference to that person. This advice had the practical effect of taking the patient out of himself. He now had to think of what somebody else wanted in order to figure out just what to do for them.

In my own practice I have found this a valuable tool for couples who have drifted apart and miss the feelings of closeness they remember having earlier in their relationship. It is also a successful tool in sex therapy, relieving inhibiting feelings of self-consciousness by getting each partner involved in pleasing the other. (Sex therapy is recent, but the principle invoked isn't: the most intensely pleasurable sex happens when your partner is intensely pleased.)

Altruism may not be in vogue nowadays, but from my experience a giver receives as many benefits as the recipient. Generosity is a healing, expansive, *happy* state of mind. I'm sure scientists will discover that, along with smiling and laughter, it releases good chemicals inside us, generating more good feelings.

And now a word for the benefits of negativity—just to keep a balanced view. I have said that the depths of human negativity have yet to be plumbed. In this respect, I have seen people carry out monumentally hard decisions just to *spite* the lack of support from family and friends. Basically, people are capable of using any reaction as a source of strength. If the resolve to carry out the decision is there, lack of support can even be experienced as supportive.

Annie has told me that quite a few A.A. members have profited by a *lack* of support in staying sober. "When I joined A.A. my wife said I'd be drunk again within three weeks—a prediction I remembered every time I wanted a drink, from the day I got sober until the desire to drink finally left me. I was so mad, I'd have died before I picked up that drink."

Annie also told me about Emily, an A.A. friend whose mother was "dragged" to Alanon, the support group for family members of alcoholics. Emily had resorted to strong-arm tactics because her mother, Faith, a feisty eighty-two-year-old who should have been a general or chairman of a board at least, had spent her life whipping her two children into shape—only to watch them disintegrate into alcoholic wrecks eluding her control.

When Emily recovered in A.A., she could see clearly what was happening to her brother and how his alcoholism was affecting Faith. Faith's denial of her son's manipulations and her own need for Alanon was monumental, but Emily turned the control tables and marched her off to a meeting anyway.

Faith soon exchanged her negativity for activity in the local Alanon groups and even began to curb her controlling instincts enough to give her son room to start dealing with his alcoholism. But the fringe benefit turned out to be a whole new group of friends for a woman who had been very lonely—Faith had outlived so many of her friends that her social circle had become smaller and smaller.

"She started planning her funeral when she was seventy-two," Emily said. "I even remember a ghoulish meeting with a funeral director who got more and more depressed as my mother chattered on about her funeral. She made him quote her the cheapest price on coffins and ordered cremation. Then she said we wouldn't need to rent one of his rooms for a memorial service—because, as a church member, she got one free. 'I think just the chapel, off the main chancel, since most of my friends are gone now, don't you think, dear?'

"Ten years—and Alanon—later, the whole picture had changed. 'Of course I'll need the whole church,' she told me not long ago. 'Maybe we could have the choir sing. I've always liked *Amazing Grace* . . . There'll be upwards of sixty people there, what do you think we should serve after the ceremony? Coffee and cake?'" Apparently, going to a support group for a particular problem can lead to support and friendship in all areas of your life—or, as in the case of Faith, post-life parties.

My co-author found unexpected support from strangers along the side of the road—quite literally. "I entered a race in New York's Central Park last January, thinking that if I had two thousand other people running with me I might make it for five miles without stopping. I've never participated in sports, so it never occurred to me that anyone would still be at the finish line, watching me shuffle in. Well, I got a kind of support I'd never experienced—they were cheering me! I loved it."

She kept on training and running in longer races. ("More cheers.") Since she was training for the New York Marathon while working on this book, there were times when she wondered if she hadn't overreacted to this intoxicating form of support. "Just this once—and never, never again," she found herself muttering when she forced herself to return to the typewriter after a fifteen-mile training run. "I've learned my lesson." We'll see. I have good reason to believe that cheers and support can be habit forming.

The fact is, there are many strangers out there willing to give you their support, just as your friends are probably willing to support you—if only you will tell people what you want. My office fills up with patients because people know they can tell me what they want without feeling guilty, because they pay me, and maybe someone has recommended me as an old curmudgeon who'll listen.

I don't want to discourage anyone from coming to me, because I find my work very satisfying. But I do know that giving support is every bit as enriching as receiving it. Asking for support isn't the same thing as asking people to do the work for you—I don't do that for my patients, and your friends can't solve your problems, either.

But it is a great gift to share your intentions and plans for achieving your goals with others. It is a great gift to allow them to participate in your life by supporting your efforts—even if only with a cheer or a smile of encouragement.

It's the connection between all of us that counts.

10

"I Want to Be a Part of Life; I Want to Be Happy"

I read everything I can on decisions, so I have some interesting tangential material. For instance, a study of heredity and schizophrenia revealed that if one schizophrenic is an identical twin, there's an 80 percent chance the other twin will become schizophrenic, too. What intrigues me is: What about the other 20 percent?

I looked into it and found out that, yes, there is an inherited tendency toward schizophrenia in that 20 percent. In addition, the early experience of the 20 percent people provided them with the kind of environment and circumstances in which schizophrenia can flourish. But *the non-schizophrenic twins simply decided that they didn't want to be crazy.* They decided they wanted to find some other way of dealing with their problems.

I have often found people who will remember a moment when they decided to go crazy or, like the twins in the 20 percent, decided to stay sane. Even institutionalized psychotics can often remember this moment.

A common reason why people decide to be crazy is that it seems a less damaging choice than to kill or to commit suicide.

Another common situation is this: in the interest of getting even with his parents, a child may choose to go crazy. This way he can express his overwhelming anger, which seems murderous to him, and at the same time remain a nice person. By retreating into insanity he builds a nice safe wall around his rage. The negative payoff, of course, is monumental.

I want to share one last case history with you. It illustrates just about everything I've learned about the role of decision in our lives—and, also, will introduce you to a truly unforgettable character.

Mental hospitals have a special smell—disinfectants not really masking the lingering odors of urine and sweat and food flung into corners, a sort of zoo smell. But the smell that really triggers an escape response is the smell of fear: the fear of going crazy or the fear of going sane. They both smell the same in a mental hospital.

And the hospitals in Scandinavia smell the same as the ones in the United States. I was about to demonstrate Direct Decision Therapy to the staff of a mental hospital in a small town in Norway. I had asked for a volunteer from the inmates, one who could speak English.

The patient shambling toward me looked like a typical, hopeless, back-ward schizophrenic. Her shapeless bathrobe was food stained, her hair stringy and uncombed. Her body was puffy and soft from years of institutional food and lack of exercise. She couldn't have been more than twenty, but the look of shell shock from internal battles had left her face haggard and worn. Her eyes, however, were wildly active.

I gestured toward a chair. "Won't you sit down, please?"

"When I'm ready. I'll sit when I'm ready."

"Would you tell me your name?"

She waved an arm toward the staff member seated behind me. "You heard him. Marie, my name is MARIE!"

"I'm sorry, Marie, I didn't catch it at first. Now I wonder if there is anything I can do for you. Would you like me to help you?"

"You can't help me, none of you can help me. Why don't you *leave me alone*? WHY ARE YOU ALWAYS AT ME . . ."

She rushed on, shouting at the top of her voice and using a

mixture of expletives and obscenities that showed an admirable command of English as well as Norwegian.

Nothing I could do could make the situation any worse, so I decided to try something drastic. I outshouted her.

"CUT IT OUT, MARIE! YOU KNOW YOU DON'T HAVE TO TALK LIKE THAT."

She stopped suddenly and focused on me for the first time. The muscles in her face relaxed ever so slightly, and her eyes showed awareness and intelligence.

"How'd you know?"

I stared at her for a minute, giving her my best foxy-grandpa look. "It takes one to know one," I said finally—at which point Marie's face broke into a grin.

"You mean *you're* crazy? You too?"

"Perhaps. And perhaps the only difference between you and me is that I know how to act sane."

Marie seemed to like the sound of that. She tightened the sash of her bathrobe and sat down.

"So," I went on, "what do you want? Do you think I can help you?"

"Yes. You can get me out of this crazy place."

"Are you sure you want out?"

"Yes."

"If you really want to get out, Marie, you'll have to make a very simple decision."

"What's that?"

"Decide to act sane. You can start by answering some questions I need to ask you."

I watched her face. Suspicion again. Then, again, that almost imperceptible relaxation of tiny facial muscles.

"When did you decide to go crazy, Marie?"

Now came another grin. "That's such an easy question, I don't know why nobody ever asked me before. When I was five years old. My mother was screaming at me about something, and as usual I just shut my eyes and put my hands over my ears—I hated it so. This time she got so furious that she said, 'You're crazy.' So I said to myself, if you think I'm crazy now, I'll show you crazy.

"After that I was terrible. I wouldn't listen to her or look at her. I got worse and worse. She took me to every doctor in town, I really was driving *her* crazy. But she never listened to me—so why should I speak understandably to her? Then I talked so crazy she started sending me to hospitals. This is the third one I've been in."

"Are you sure you want to give this up, Marie?"

"What do you mean?"

"I want to know what you're getting out of acting crazy. What's the payoff?"

"Oh, I see." She leaned back in the chair and crossed her legs. She was beginning to enjoy herself. "Of course I get things out of it. For one, I never have to look after myself if I don't want to. I can stay here, and they'll take care of me for the rest of my life. Another thing is, I don't have to look for a job. The third thing is, I don't have to listen to my mother say, 'Why don't you go out like other girls?' There are enough crazy guys here, and we get together and have a good time.

"And best of all, I get to say whatever I feel like saying to my mother. I could even kill her if I wanted to. After all, I'm crazy."

This last remark made everybody laugh, probably because every doctor in the room knew it was true.

"I can see those are terrific payoffs," I said when the laughter had died down. "Now what I want to know is, why would you want to give them up?"

Marie's expression changed. Gone was the cockiness; in its place I saw hope mingled with fear.

"I want to be a part of life." She was quiet for a long moment, then she went on. "Yes. I'm sick and tired of all this. I want to be a part of life. I want to be happy."

"Then I can tell you what to do," I said, "if that's what you really want."

"It's what I really want."

"All you have to do, Marie, is decide to act sane. Do you think you can do that?"

"Sure," she said with a smile. "I'm scheduled for a weekend home. I'm going to go there and act sane."

"All right, Marie. Now what do you think will happen when you go home and you act sane with your family?"

"They'll be overjoyed."

I shook my head. "All I can say is that, from my experience, I don't think so. I want you to act sane since that's what you decided to do, but don't expect your family to be overjoyed. Remember, they're used to you acting crazy. Which may not make it easy for you to act sane."

"I can do it. I've tried everything else in that house."

I came back to the hospital a few days after Marie's weekend.

"How did it go, Marie?"

"You must know my family. When I told them what we had decided—that I should act sane—my mother started to cry and my sister starts shouting, 'She was bad enough before, now that American professor's driven her *really* crazy.'" Marie sighed. "And I was really acting very sane, saner than she was acting."

"She'll get over it," I said. "The important thing is, you stuck to your choice."

Marie already looked different. She had taken some care with her clothes and hair; best of all, her whole expression was one of aliveness. She wasn't particularly pleased with what was happening, but she wasn't ready to retreat into the quicksand of madness.

It would be all too easy to conclude that Marie had been faking her illness for all those years. She had not. When she entered my classroom the week before, she wasn't acting schizophrenic. She *was* schizophrenic. When as a child she stopped talking so that anyone could understand her, she had stopped relating to the reality around her. (She had stopped listening, too.) Severing connections to reality is dangerous, because they are so hard to reconnect. And there is always the temptation to loosen again when life gets particularly difficult or frightening.

Marie hung on to my advice, perhaps because I had met her part way across the abyss. First she heard *my* shouting, then she listened to my description of "crazy" and "sane" as acts. The instant she dropped her crazy mask and declared that she wanted to go out in the world, she created one of those "teachable moments" I've talked about. The force of the truth opened her up and made her receptive to new information. My advice to her—stop acting crazy, start acting sane—made sense in terms of her present reality and in terms of the new reality she was already searching for. All of which is why, from the moment of decision on, she was able to start reclaiming control over her life.

I was fortunate enough to see Marie several more times that year. On one particularly memorable occasion, I was giving a workshop on psychotherapy in which Marie had offered to be a subject for a demonstration. The topic was rage and fantasy. Marie was extraordinarily imaginative in devising various ways of killing her mother. At one point she came up with chopping up Mom and carefully cutting her into bite-size pieces to fry with onions for her father's dinner.

Marie enjoyed this performance enormously—and not just because she enjoyed the response of the class. She realized that even the most diabolical fantasy has no power to harm. She saw that she didn't have to act crazy in order to be angry—that feelings are not facts.

Marie also discovered in herself a toughness, a resiliency that gave her the strength to stick with her decision to act sane. It wasn't easy, either. "If I had known *how* hard it is to be sane" (she wrote me when she finally got out of the hospital for good), "how lonely it is to be out here, and if I could have gotten my hands on you, I would have kicked your ass right into a straitjacket."

Marie lived in the small town next to the hospital, and for a while I kept getting reports from the staff that she had found an effective outlet for venting her frustrations and anger over being "out there." She gave long discourses to anyone who would listen about what a rat I was for having gotten her involved in the outside world.

The whole town got a course on decisions, including the negative payoffs for Marie's. They were told to watch out for people like me, tricking you into making a decision so you have to do all the work, etc. Her diatribes were always entertaining, and the townspeople became an appreciative audience. I could see that Marie was getting payoffs for devising ingenious ways to make me pay for her increasing sanity.

Before long she made another decision—to go to university. There, she withdrew into herself for a period. She had never been in a completely strange environment before. People in her town had been exposed to Marie, acting crazy or acting sane, all her life.

She wrote to describe her reaction to her first social occasion. "The fact is, I don't know how to talk to people my own age, or what to talk about. After all, I've been cloistered away like some nun. I've been away from the world so many years, I really don't know how to act."

I saw her a few months later and asked her what she was doing these days about social occasions.

"I try to keep quiet, mostly. I don't want people to know how crazy I was. All that stuff is depressing, and I don't want people to feel sorry for me. So I just don't say much of anything."

"That's one solution," I said, "but it may not be the only one.

Why don't you tell people the truth about how crazy you were?
You could do it in such a way as to show them how naturally funny
you are. You have wonderful stories, I know, about the hospital.
No one will feel sorry for you if you make them laugh. They'll just
think you're terrific."

In her next letter, she wrote that she had been the star of the
show at parties ever since trying out my advice. I wasn't surprised;
I knew Marie was a performer at heart. I also knew her courage
and comic abilities would win her many new friends.

A year later, Marie wrote me from the mountains, where she was
backpacking with a friend. She had run across a psychiatrist from
the mental hospital—who hadn't recognized her. He just couldn't
connect this healthy, attractive young woman (with her boyfriend
in tow) to the paranoid schizophrenic who had lived for so long in
his hospital.

Marie eventually married and had a child. When the baby was
three months old, she wrote:

"When she was born, I began to find life too much for me. I not
only had to take care of her and my husband, but I still had my
studies as well. I really wanted that degree.

"I found myself beginning to drift off, drift out of my life, the
way I used to. And—I didn't! I decided to be the kind of person,
the kind of wife and mother, that I want to be. Not perfect, just
what's possible. And if I drift off, I won't be able to hear my
daughter, I'll be just like my mother was with me."

Marie grew stronger and more sure of herself with each decision
to reinforce her present reality by paying attention and not "drifting off." And her talent for self-parody and her gift of repartee
came to her aid when she was down. She could always make people
laugh—and then she would join them. We talked about this as an
effective release for her fears and frustrations. Not surprisingly,
she was wonderfully creative at painting word pictures of herself so
droll that she herself found them ludicrous. Her ability with words

even led her to writing for a time, where she found a certain amount of success and satisfaction as a copywriter.

But her final choice of profession led her, in a way, back to the mental hospital. For Marie was not only amazingly perceptive about herself, she had a real gift for perceiving other people. She also had the desire to be useful in the world, to help people. And so, after considering various alternatives, Marie decided to study to be a psychologist. I feel reasonably sure that Marie's own experiences will have equipped her all the better to understand other people's suffering.

First, Marie was a patient full of surprises (the kind of patient I find most challenging). Then she was a long-distance friend whose letters were entertaining, enlightening, even inspiring. Now I can look forward to having her as a colleague likely to make creative contributions to our field.

Marie has asked that I include in this book a brief essay she sent me describing our experience together as she sees it. I treasure this letter, though I have a somewhat different view of its subject. To me, it's a description of Marie's experience with the good therapist in herself.

The Ringmaster

Actually he was not that. It was only a name they called him. For he loved strong effects, things outside the program, laughter. He never even flinched from ridiculing himself, if only it could bring him nearer his target.

Actually he was a professor. But what serious professor would accept to be called by a circus name? To be joked about, even if fondly? But his colleagues recognized his talent and were eager to learn from him. For with all sorts of magician's tricks and flourishes, he got the patients on his side in the fight against their illness.

"I am just as crazy as you," he could say. Then the patient might wonder if being sane might be stranger than being crazy.

He came into our dark and closed world and pulled hope and laughter out of his top hat. He didn't conceal what it would cost to be on his side of the lights, to struggle toward health. But always the patients knew that he had led troupes of them out before—into the bright center ring, into the real, tough world. If it is tough for the average person, it is even tougher for the one coming from the mental hospital. Some turned back: the darkness is a good friend.

But he got results, results nobody had thought possible. Nobody except himself—he believed in us, he believed the possibilities he saw in us. And so he took risks and led us out into the center ring, even onto the high wire. But he never asked us to take risks he wouldn't take himself.

This patient and the Ringmaster became friends. Such good friends that she started to look at herself as a star number in his circus. The two of them pitted their wits against each other at seminars where the participants forgot their dignity and laughed.

She never knew what would happen next when she talked to him. She might suddenly find herself flying through the air, on the swings of chance. For he taught her to trust herself.

She has met other professors, but to her he is the greatest of them all. For it is he who stepped down from the pedestal of authority and came into her world, as an equal. Perhaps that is the key to his magical results.

Once again, a patient comes up with the right answers for herself and gives me the credit for her own wisdom. I am so often the beneficiary of such enormous generosity.

Like Marie, we all, even the most miserable of us, have the capacity for happiness. Many choose to escape from life; many others immerse themselves in it—with joy. Marie's choice is very clear: "I want to be a part of life. I want to be happy."

Appendix A

A Short Form of Direct Decision Therapy

I want to leave you with a short form of Direct Decision Therapy in case you want to ask yourself seven quick questions.

Step I: Decide what you want in order to be happy
Step II: Find the decision behind the problem
Step III: Find the context for the original decision
Step IV: List the payoffs for the decision
Step V: Examine your alternatives to the behavior that's causing the problem
Step VI: Choose your alternative and decide to put it into practice
Step VII: Support yourself in carrying out your decision

Appendix B

Support Groups

THERE are self-help networks and support groups for every problem conceivable, but since new ones are being formed and others may be in address transitions, the best way to find out how to contact, or if need be to form, one in your community is to phone your local Self-Help Clearinghouse. If you fail to find one listed in your phone book write or phone:

> National Self-Help Clearinghouse
> 33 West 42nd Street, Room 1206A
> New York, NY 10036
> Tel: 212 840-7606

The National Institute of Mental Health, a division of the Department of Human Services, has prepared a fact sheet on self-help groups. It is available at no charge from:

> Consumer Information Center
> Department 609K
> Pueblo
> Colorado 81009